S0-AIC-931

1492

*THE DEBATE ON COLONIALISM,
EUROCENTRISM, AND HISTORY*

1492

THE DEBATE ON COLONIALISM, EUROCENTRISM, AND HISTORY

J. M. Blaut

with contributions by

Andre Gunder Frank
Samir Amin
Robert A. Dodgshon
Ronen Palan

Africa World Press, Inc.

P.O. Box 1892
Trenton, New Jersey 08607

Africa World Press, Inc.
P.O. Box 1892
Trenton, NJ 08607

Copyright © Butterworth-Heinemann, 1992
First Africa World Press Inc., Edition, 1992

All rights reserved. No part of this publication may be reproduced, stored in a retrieval system or transmitted in any form or by any means electronic, mechanical, photocopying, recording or otherwise without the prior written permission of the publisher.

The essays in this book were first published in the journal Political Geography (Peter J. Taylor, editor), vol. 11, no. 4, July 1992, as a debate 'On the Significance of 1492', and appears in this book through the courtesy of the publishers, Butterworth-Heinemann 1992

Map on the cover is reproduced from *Aramco World*, May–June 1992.
Cover Design by Carles Juzang
Book design by Jonathan Gullery
This book is composed in New Century Schoolbook

Library of Congress Cataloging-in-Publication Data

Blaut, James M. (James Morris)
    1492 : the debate on colonialism, Eurocentrism, and history /
James M. Blaut with contributions by Andre Gunder Frank ... [et al.].
        p.   cm.
    Includes bibliographical references and index.
    ISBN 0-86543-369-0 (hard back). -- ISBN 0-86543-370-4 (pbk.)
    1. Economic history. 2. Europe--Economic conditions--16th century.
3. Europe--Colonies--America. 4. Capitalism--Europe-History. I. Title.
    HC51.B64 1992
    330.9--dc20
                                                            92-32975
                                                            CIP

Contents

Foreword: A Debate on the Significance of 1492

Peter J. Taylor

University of Newcastle upon Tyne

Introduction

Some published debates work, others don't. This one belongs firmly in the former category. The journal *Political Geography* has published a variety of public debates in recent years of which the one reproduced here is the latest. The format used is a simple one. There is a main paper by Jim Blaut which strongly expresses a controversial thesis. There are four commentators, two of whom are broadly sympathetic to the thesis (Gunder Frank and Samir Amin) and two who disagree with it (Bob Dodgshon and Ronen Palan). Finally Blaut is given the opportunity to comment on the commentators.

There are two main reasons why this debate is so successful. First there is the quality of the contributions — be prepared to be persuaded by some quite contrary positions! Second the question being debated is a very big one with crucial implications for how we view the world we live in. It is for this reason that, as editor of *Political Geography*, I am delighted that this particular debate is reaching a larger audience than the *aficionados* of the journal. The main protagonist Jim Blaut has asked me to contribute this short introduction to the republication and I decided to accept only if I could add some value to the product. Obviously it would be inappropriate for me to join in the debate at this late stage, not to mention unfair to the other contributors, but I thought it would be useful for readers if I attempted to place the debate into some sort of context. I have already stated that I believe the debate to be an important one; it is now incumbent upon me to say why.

All Historical Geography Is Myth

All history that is worth reading is contested history. Any writer who thinks she or he has 'settled' some historical question is more interesting for what they represent than for what they say. To me the phrase contested history initially brings to mind the 'battle of memoirs and autobiographies' that often occurs between 'great men' trying to ensure their place for posterity. But there is much more to historical debate than such purposive bias. Wallerstein (1983) has asserted that all history is myth. By this he means that all historians bring to their subject matter a set of assumptions about how the world works which determines the nature of the historical knowledge which they produce. Hence different historians starting from different positions each produce their different 'myths'.

Wallerstein uses the very strong word 'myth' to emphasize his distance from those who believe in the possibility of producing an 'absolute truth'. In history the latter are best represented by the Whig historians of the era of British hegemony who thought that they could eventually produce an 'ultimate history' when the 'last fact' was finally interpreted (Carr, 1961). There are two key challenges to such thinking. The first argues that all history is a dialogue between the past and the present where the contemporary concerns of the historians define the questions asked of the past (Carr, 1961). It can be no other way:

we are trapped in the present. Hence we now interpret the
Whig historical project with its emphasis on continuity
and progress culminating in the present as a celebration,
and hence legitimation, of the present. 'Now' is made a
'special time'.

The second challenge argues that the position an historian starts from needs to be specified much more pre-
cisely than merely the present. As with other cultural
pursuits, historians have been in the business of what
Rana Kabbani (1988) calls 'devise and rule'. The present
is the modern and the modern is a place, the 'West'. 'Here'
— where the historian comes from — is made a 'special
place'. There is a geographical dialogue between places,
just as inherently biassed as the historian's one between
times, in all descriptions of our world (Taylor, 1993). In
fact much geographical writing has been more like a geographical monologue as the 'moderns' have scripted the
'pre-moderns' in keeping them in their place. Hence we
can say that all historical geography — understanding the
times and places of our world — is a myth. The debate con-
ducted here is above all about choosing between alternative historical geography myths; it is about trying to think
beyond the here and now.

The Greatest *Ossian* of Them All?

The controversial position that Blaut proposes may be
described as characterizing most world history as a 'great
Ossian'. The *Ossian* was an epic poem that purported to
show that the flowering of medieval Celtic culture occurred
in the Highlands of Scotland and not Ireland as commonly supposed (Trevor-Roper, 1983). It was an eighteenth
century romantic nationalist forgery that was trying to
induce a rewriting of Celtic historical geography: a peripheral region was being promoted to centre stage putting
its more illustrious rival in the shade. In similar manner
standard world histories can be characterized as making
what was until fairly recently a rather peripheral part of

a loose 'world-system', Europe, into a special place where
progress is to be found. This is not to say the world historians have purposively forged the evidence as in the original *Ossian*, but the results of their less purposive bias
have had the same effect except on a much grander scale.
In their slightly different ways, Blaut, Frank and Amin
make *Ossian*-type accusations; Dodgshon and Palan
doubt, on somewhat different grounds, whether down-
grading the special or unique nature of Europe aids our
understanding of the modern world.

I am not going to describe the five positions argued
below any further than locating them in the context just
provided. What I can promise the readers is a very rich
debate and I would suggest that they would be hard put
to find the equivalent concentration of ideas in any other
publication of comparable length.

Who Has Got the Best Myth?

This is the question the reader is being invited to
answer. But answering is not just a matter of assembling
the facts to decide. There is an important sense in which
facts should be respected and not manipulated unfairly
but that is not the prime issue here. It is much more basic
than that. It seems to me that neither side could put
together a set of facts that would satisfy the other side they
were proven wrong: 'I'm sorry, you were right all along...'.
We are in the realm of interpretation and that is encum-
bered by the historiographical assumptions described earlier. But you, the reader, carry such assumptions around
in your head. Nobody reading this debate will come to it
as an 'intellectual blank'; you will have either celebrated
or mourned the events of 1492 this year and that will
indelibly mark your reading of the debate. Nevertheless
it is always a refreshing exercise to read other people's
myth even though reading 'your side's' rebuttals is more
reassuring.

But where does all this subjectivity leave us? There may

be no absolute truth but we do not want to be pushed into an extreme 'relativist' position where every myth is as good as every other and we just pick the one that suits us. There are criteria for selecting between myths. It has to do with what the selector's purpose is in making her or his choice. If it is a scholarly choice then we will need to take particular heed of the facts. But facts themselves don't just appear for us to collect; our theories lead us to our facts. But our theories are ultimately about how our world works and that is political. Hence the criteria used in this debate to select a preferred myth will be ultimately political.

For my part I think history is not about the past, or even the present, but its prime reference is the future. That was the message of the old Whig histories just as much as new radical histories. I also think geography is not about 'foreign places', or even our home place, but its prime space reference is the whole world. That was the message of the old imperialist geographies just as much as new radical geographies. Hence historical geography and its myths are about the future of the world. That is the space-time context of the debate presented here.

References

Carr, E. H. (1961). *What Is History?* London: Penguin.

Kabbani, R. (1988). *Europe's Myth of Orient*. London: Pandora.

Taylor, P. J. (1993). Full circle, or new meaning for the global? In *The Challenge For Geography* (R. J. Johnston, ed.). Oxford: Blackwell.

Trevor-Roper, H. (1983). The invention of tradition: The highland tradition in Scotland. In *The Invention of Tradition* (E. Hobsbawm and T. Ranger, eds.). Cambridge: Cambridge University Press.

Wallerstein, I. (1983). *Historical Capitalism*. London: Verso.

Fourteen Ninety-two

J. M. Blaut

*University of Illinois
at Chicago*

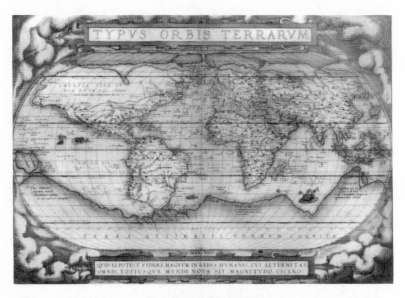

Introduction

Five hundred years have passed since Europeans arrived in America, yet we still don't fully realize how significant that event was for cultural evolution. I am going to argue in this essay that the date 1492 represents the breakpoint between two fundamentally different evolutionary epochs. The conquest of America begins, and explains, the rise of Europe. It explains why capitalism rose to power in Europe, not elsewhere, and why capitalism rose to power in the 17th century, not later. Fourteen ninety-two gave the world a center and a periphery.

Before 1492, cultural evolution in the Eastern Hemisphere was proceeding evenly across the landscape; in Africa, Asia, and Europe a multitude of centers were evolving out of (broadly) feudalism and toward (broadly) capitalism. Many of these regions in all three continents were at the same level of development and were progressing at about the same rate and (as to their modes of production) in the same direction. They were in fact evolving collectively, as nodes in a hemisphere-wide network or process of evolving capitalism. Europe was not in any way ahead of Africa and Asia in development or even in the preconditions for development.

After 1492, Europeans came to dominate the world, and they did so because 1492 inaugurated a set of world-historical processes which gave to European protocapitalists enough capital and power to dissolve feudalism in their own region and begin the destruction of competing protocapitalist communities everywhere else. By the end of the 17th century, two hundred years after 1492, capitalism (or capitalists) had risen to take political and social control of a few Western European countries, and colonial expansion had decisively begun in Africa and Asia. Europe was now beginning to dominate the world and to lead the world in level and pace of development. The world's landscapes were now uneven. They have remained so ever since.

Nobody doubts that the discovery and exploitation of America by Europeans had something to do with the rise and modernization of Europe. What I am arguing here is a much stronger and much more radical thesis. The argument is radical in at least four respects.

(1) It denies that Europeans had *any* advantage over Africans and Asians prior to 1492 as regards the evolutionary processes leading toward capitalism and modernity. Medieval Europe was no more advanced or

progressive than medieval Africa and medieval Asia, and had no special potentialities — no unique gift of 'rationality' or 'venturesomeness'.

(2) I am at the same time asserting that colonialism, as a process, lies at the heart (not at the periphery) of such world-historical transformations as the rise of capitalism and Europe. Capitalism would (I suspect) have arrived in any case, but it would have arrived many centuries later and it would not have seated itself in Europe alone (or first) had it not been for European colonialism in America. Later colonialism was crucial to the later evolution of capitalism (a thesis I cannot pursue in this short essay). Colonialism, overall, has been a crucial dimension of capitalism from 1492 down to the present.

(3) I am arguing that the economic exploitation of Americans in the 16th and 17th centuries was vastly more intensive, and produced vastly more capital, than is generally recognized. The argument then moves to Europe, and claims — following somewhat the lead of earlier writers like E.J. Hamilton (1929) and W.P. Webb (1951) — that economic, social, and political effects of colonial accumulation, principally in America, produced a major transformation of European society.

(4) I am parting company with those traditional Marxists who, like traditional conservatives, believe that the rise of capitalism is to be explained by processes internal to Europe. Strictly speaking, there was no 'transition from feudalism to capitalism' in Europe; there was rather a sharp break, a historical unconformity, between medieval Europe and the Europe of the bourgeois revolution (or revolutions). That unconformity appears in the historical column just in 1492. After 1492 we see sudden, revolutionary change. There was no European transition in still another sense. A transition toward capitalism and from a range of broadly feudal and feudal-tributary modes of production was indeed taking place before 1492, but it was taking place on a hemisphere-wide scale. All of the Marxist models which

attempt to discover causality within an intra-European
system only — the decline of rural *feudalism* in Europe
(Brenner, 1976, 1977, 1982); the rise of European towns
(Sweezy, 1976) — are deficient because the real causality is hemisphere-wide in extent and effect.

In the following paragraphs I will present the reasoning behind these propositions. The plan of procedure is as
follows. To begin with, I will try to show that our magnif-
icent legacy of European historical scholarship does not
provide important evidence against the theory argued here
because it is not really comparative. I will show that the
basic reason why we have accepted the idea of European
historical superiority is Eurocentric diffusionism, thus a
matter of methodology, ideology, and implicit theory, not
empirical evidence. Next, I will try to show that Europe
was at about the same level as Africa and Asia in 1492,
that a common process of evolution toward capitalism was
occurring in a network of regions across the hemisphere.
This argument, still a preliminary to our main thesis (but
an essential step in laying out the overall theory), will be
put forward in two brief discussions. First I will very
sketchily summarize and criticize the views of a number
of scholars who maintain that Europe was indeed more
advanced and progressive than other regions in the Middle
Ages. Then I will sketch in the empirical basis for the
opposing theory, that of evenness prior to 1492, here sum-
marizing prior reports (principally Blaut, 1976). We then
arrive at the main argument, which is a presentation of
empirical evidence that colonialism after 1492 led to the
massive accumulation of capital (and protocapitalist
power) in Europe, and so explains why Europe began its
selective rise and experienced, in the 17th century, its
political transformation, the bourgeois revolutions. In the
course of this discussion I will show that the discovery of
America and the beginnings of colonialism did not reflect
any superiority of Europe over Africa or Asia, but rather
reflected the facts of location.

Prior Questions

The Question of Evidence

Libraries are full of scholarly studies which seem to support the historical propositions which I here reject, and two of them in particular: the theory that Europe held advantages over Africa and Asia in the period prior to 1492, and the theory that the world outside of Europe had little to do with cultural evolution after 1492, and thus that colonialism was a minor and unimportant process, an effect not a cause, in world history from 1492 to the present.

But existing historical scholarship does not give much support to these theories, although this is not generally realized. Most of the support comes from unrecognized, implicit beliefs which have not been tested empirically, beliefs which are mainly an inheritance from prior times when scholars simply did not question the superiority of Europe and Europeans. Before we turn to our empirical argument it is important to demonstrate why this is so, because *no* empirical argument presented in one short essay can otherwise seem to have the power to stand up to theories which are almost universally accepted and are thought to be supported with mountains of evidence gathered by generations of scholars.

There is of course abundant historical evidence for the Middle Ages that European society was evolving and changing in many ways. From the 10th century, the changes tended to be of the sort that we can connect logically with the genuine modernization which appeared much later: towns (in some periods and places) were growing larger and more powerful, feudal society was changing in distinct ways that suggest internal change or decay, long-distance trade on land and sea was becoming more intensive and extensive, and so on. All of this is clearly shown in the scholarly record. But what does it imply for cultural evolution? And what does it *not* imply?

It does imply that a process of evolution toward some

sort of new society, probably more or less capitalist in its underlying mode of production, was underway in Europe. It does not tell us whether this evolutionary process was taking place *only* in Europe. And it does not provide us with the critical evidence which we must have to decide *why* the evolutionary changes took place in Europe, for two reasons: firstly, critical changes in Europe may have been caused by historical events which took place outside of Europe, so the facts of European history may not contain the causes of evolutionary change; and secondly, for any postulated cause of an evolutionary change in Europe, if the same process (or fact) occurred outside of Europe but did not, there, produce the same effect as it did in Europe, we have good reason to doubt that this particular fact or process was causally efficacious within Europe. (I am using a common-sense notion of 'cause', the notion which we use pragmatically whenever we speak about causes and effects in human affairs, whatever some philosophers may say in objection.)

Of course, none of this precludes the spinning of grand historical theories as to what caused evolutionary change in European society at any given period in history, before 1492 or after. My point is that such theories cannot be proven; they do not rest in the factual evidence but rather in *a priori* beliefs about the causes of historical change. The mountain of factual evidence does not really help us to decide whether causes are economic, or political, or intellectual, or technological, or whatever. We can weave these facts into almost any sort of explanatory model. But we cannot prove our case. In sum, our great heritage of careful, scholarly studies about European history does not, by itself, provide evidence against any theory which claims that the causal forces which were at work in Europe were also at work elsewhere.

Diffusionism and Tunnel History

There is one primordial reason why we do not doubt that Europeans have taken the lead in history, in all epochs before and after 1492, and it has little to do with evidence. It is a basic belief which we inherit from prior ages of thought and scarcely realize that we hold: it is an *implicit* belief, not an explicit one, and it is so large a theory that it is woven into *all* of our ideas about history, both within Europe and without. This is the theory, or super-theory, called Eurocentric diffusionism (Blaut, 1977, 1987a).

Diffusionism is a complex doctrine, with a complex history, but the essence is clear. It became codified around the middle of the 19th century as part of the ideology of evolving capitalism in Europe, but more specifically because it gave powerful intellectual support to colonialism. Its basic propositions are the following:

(1) It is natural and normal to find cultural evolution progressing within Europe.

(2) The prime reason for cultural evolution within Europe is some force or factor which is ultimately intellectual or spiritual, a source of inventiveness (the inventions being social as well as technological), rationality, innovativeness, and virtue.

(3) Outside of Europe, cultural progress is not to be expected: the norm is stagnation, 'traditionalism', and the like.

(4) Progress outside of Europe reflects diffusion from Europe of traits (in the aggregate 'civilization') invented in Europe.

(5) The natural form of interaction between Europe and non-Europe is a transaction: the diffusion of innovative ideas, values, and people from Europe to non-Europe; the counter-diffusion of material wealth, as just compensation, from non-Europe to Europe. (There is also a different kind of counter-diffusion, from periphery to core, which consists of things backward, atavistic, and uncivilized: black magic, plagues, barbarians, Dracula, etc., this being a natural consequence of the fact that the periphery is ancient, backward, and savage.)

Thus in essence: Europe invents, others imitate; Europe advances, others follow (or they are led).

Certainly the primary argument of diffusionism is the

superiority of Europeans over non-Europeans, and the conception that history outside of Europe is made by the diffusion from Europe of Europeans and their intellectual and moral inventions. But the internal, or core, part of the model is critical when we try to analyze the ways (real) Europeans theorize about their own history and their own society, past and present. This part of diffusionism combines two doctrines (derived from diffusionist propositions no. 1 and no. 2) which involve a kind of historical tunnel-vision, and so can be called 'tunnel history' (Blaut, 1987b, chap. 7, and forthcoming). The first doctrine declares it unnecessary to look outside of Europe for the causes of historical changes in Europe (except of course decivilizing changes like barbarian invasions, plagues, heresies, etc.). Historical reasoning thus looks back or down the tunnel of time for the causes of all important changes: outside the tunnel is the rockbound, changeless, traditional periphery, the non-European world. This becomes a definite methodology in European medieval history. Prior generations of historians did not seriously look outside of Europe, except to make invidious comparisons. If European historians today on some occasions try to be comparative, cross-cultural, in their efforts to explain Europe's medieval progress, the efforts almost invariably make use of older, colonial-era European analyses of non-European history, and (unsurprisingly) reproduce the older diffusionist ideas about such things as 'Asiatic stagnation', 'African savagery', and the like. (I return to this point below.) So tunnel history persists. It persists even for modern history: progress in the modern world is accomplished by Europeans, wherever they may now be settled, and by the enterprises put in place by Europeans.

The second doctrine is more subtle. Just as diffusionism claims that it is the intellectual and spiritual qualities of the European which, diffusing outward over the world, bring progress, so it claims that these qualities were the mainsprings of social evolution within Europe itself. Some qualifications, however, are needed. Two centuries ago it

was axiomatic that God and His church were the foun-
tainhead of progress. A Christian god of course will put
good ideas in the heads of Christians, particularly those
Christians who worship Him in the right way, and He will
lead His people forward to civilization. Gradually this
explicit doctrine became implicit, and Christian
Europeans were themselves seen as the sources of innovative ideas and hence evolutionary change, for reasons not
(usually) grounded in faith. Not until Marx did we have a
theory of cultural evolution which definitely placed the
prime cause of change outside the heads of Europeans, but
the habit of explaining evolutionary change by reference
to an autonomous realm of ideas or ideology, of supposedly
rational and moral innovation, remains dominant even
today because ideological-level causation is still, as it was
when Marx and Engels criticized it in *The German
Ideology*, the best rationalization for elitist social theory
(Marx and Engels, 1976). In any event, today the favoured
theories explaining the so-called 'European miracle' are
theories about Europeans' 'rationality', 'innovativeness',
and the rest. This holds true even for theories which
ground themselves in supposedly non-ideological facts,
notably technological determinism and social-structural
determinism. Technology may have caused social change
in Medieval Europe but it was the inventiveness of the
Europeans that caused the technology. Likewise social
structures, which also had to be invented.

The Question of Alternative Theories

Complementing diffusionism is a second external or
non-evidentiary source of persuasiveness for the theories
which discover European superiority in the Middle Ages
and later. This is the absence from historians' usual discourse of any competing theory. As we well know from our
doctrines about the methodology of social science, it is very
difficult to criticize, or even gain a perspective on, one theory unless you have in mind another, alternative theory.
(A theory cannot simply be 'confronted with the facts'.)

There is no shortage of such alternative theories about the rise of Europe and capitalism, before and after 1492. One is the theory offered here: that capitalism and modernity were evolving in parts of Europe, Africa, and Asia in the same general way and at the same rate up to the moment when the conquest of America gave Europe its first advantage, and that the rise of Europe, and of capitalism within Europe, thereafter was the vectorial resultant of these initial conditions, the inflowing of power from colonialism, and derivative intra-European effects.

But there are numerous other theories denying the idea of the 'European miracle'. For instance, it is argued by some Marxists that, in the 17th century, Europeans had a very minor advantage in terms of processes tending toward the rise of capitalism, an advantage which other societies had held in prior times — think of a foot-race with first one, then another runner taking the lead — but from the moment the bourgeoisie gained definitive control in northwestern Europe, no other bourgeoisie, anywhere else, could gain such control, given the explosively rapid growth and the power of capitalism, even in its preindustrial form. In a second theory, Europe managed to break out of the hemisphere-wide pattern of feudalism because of its peripheral position and rather backward character, which gave its feudal society (and class relations) a peculiar instability and hence led to a more rapid dissolution of feudalism and rise of capitalism. (See Amin, 1976, 1985.) In a third theory, Europeans had one special cultural characteristic indicating, not modernity or civilization or progressiveness, but savagery: a propensity, not shared by other Eastern Hemisphere societies, to attack, conquer, enslave, and rob other people, thus to 'rise' by predation. (This view is held by a number of very anti-European scholars. You will notice that it is the 'European miracle' theory inverted.) Still other theories could be listed. So there are alternatives to the theory of Europe's primacy. And the known facts fit these alternatives just as well (or badly) as they do the theories of European superiority.

Before Fourteen Ninety-Two

The European Miracle

The first claim which I make in this essay is that Europe had no advantage over other regions prior to 1492. I have argued this specific case elsewhere, and the argument will be briefly summarized below. However, the opposing theory is so widely argued that it is best to begin with a brief sketch of some of the better-known modern theories which assert that medieval Europe was already, in terms of cultural evolution, the leader among world cultures. My purpose in presenting these mini-critiques is specifically and only to show that this point of view is not self-evidently convincing: nothing more can be attempted, given the limitations of a short essay.

I think it unlikely that any European writer of the 19th century doubted the historical superiority of Europe. Perhaps Marx and Engels came closest to doing so. Rejecting ideological-level theories of historical causation, they speculated that Europe was the first civilization to acquire class modes of production because of its natural environment. Asia was dry; therefore Asian farming peoples had to rely on irrigation; therefore it became necessary for them to accept an overarching command structure which would allocate water and maintain waterworks, a special sort of power structure which was not truly a class state. The farming villages remained classless. The political authority was not a genuine ruling (and accumulating) class. So there was no class struggle — the Marxian motor of progress — and accordingly no evolution into slave, feudal, and capitalist modes of production. (See Marx, 1975; Engels, 1979. Engels probably abandoned this view, and the associated idea of an 'Asiatic Mode of Production', in the 1880s. See Engels, 1970.) In tropical regions nature was 'too lavish' to encourage social development (Marx, 1976: 513). Europe won, so to speak, by default. What is most important about this incorrect formulation is the fact that it does not posit an ancient and ongoing superiority of European culture or the European mind.

Most of the later Marxists and Neo-Marxists, perhaps because they were unwilling to credit Europeans with cultural or ideological or environmental or racial superiority yet had no strong alternative theory, tended to avoid the problem of explaining Europe's apparent historical priority. (See, e.g., the essays in Hilton, 1976.) Notable exceptions in this regard are Amin (1976, 1985), whose views we noted previously, and Abu-Lughod (1987-88, 1989), who argues that many parts of Europe, Asia, and Africa were at comparable levels of development in the 13th century.

Notable in a different sense are the views of Perry Anderson and Robert Brenner, whose theories are widely approved by non-Marxist social thinkers because they seem to argue to the conclusion that Marxist theory is not really different from Non-Marxist theory in its approach to the question of the rise of Europe and of capitalism, and no less friendly to Eurocentric diffusionism. (See Anderson, 1974a, 1974b; Brenner, 1976, 1977, 1982, 1986.) Anderson's formulation is quite close to that of Weber (*infra*) in its argument that Europeans of classical and feudal times were uniquely rational and analytical, and that the feudal superstructure (not the economy or class struggle) was the primary force guiding medieval Europe's unique development. Brenner's theory, which is highly influential (see, e.g., Corbridge, 1986; Hall, 1985; Baechler *et al.*, 1988), is not at all complicated. Class struggle between serfs and lords, influenced by depopulation, led to the decline of feudalism in northwestern Europe. (Brenner does not mention non-Europe and scarcely mentions southern Europe.) In most parts of northwestern Europe, the peasants won this class struggle and became in essence petty landowners, now satisfied with their bucolic existence and unwilling to innovate. Only in England did the lords maintain their grip on the land; peasants thus remained tenants. The peasantry then became differentiated, producing a class of landless labourers and a rising class of larger tenant farmers, wealthy enough to rent substantial holdings and forced (because they had to pay rent) to commercialize, innovate technologically, and thus become capitalists. (Brenner thinks that serfs, lords, and landowning peasants did not innovate, and that towns, even English towns, had only a minor role in the rise of capitalism.) English yeoman-tenant-farmers, therefore, were the founders of capitalism. Stated differently: capitalism arose because English peasants lost the class struggle. In reality, peasants were not predominantly landowners in the other countries of the region; capitalism grew more rapidly in and near the towns than in the rural countryside; and the technological innovativeness which Brenner attributes to 14th-15th century English farmers really occurred much later, too late to fit into his theory. More importantly, commercial farming and indeed urban protocapitalism were developing during this period in southern Europe and (as I will argue) in other continents. Brenner's theory is simply wrong. Its popularity is due principally to two things. First, put forward as a Marxist view, grounded in class struggle, it proves to be, on inspection, a theory that is fairly standard, if somewhat rural in bias. It seems to follows that class-struggle theories lead to conventional conclusions. And secondly, Brenner uses his theory (1977: 77-92) to attack the unpopular 'Third-Worldist' perspectives of dependency theory, underdevelopment theory, and in particular Sweezy, Frank, and Wallerstein, who argue that European colonialism had much to do with the later rise of capitalism. (See Frank, 1967; Wallerstein, 1974.) Brenner is a thoroughgoing Eurocentric tunnel historian: non-Europe had no important role in social evolution at any historical period. Unaware that colonialism involves capitalist relations of production — see below — he claims that the extra-European world merely had commercial effects on Europe, whereas the rise of capital-

ism was in no way a product of commerce: it took place
in the countryside of England and reflected class strug-
gle, not trade. (See critiques of Brenner by R. Hilton, P.
Croot and D. Parker, H. Wunder, E. LeRoy Ladurie, G.
Bois, J.P. Cooper, and others collected in Aston and
Philpin, 1985. See Torras, 1980; Hoyle, 1990.)

Certainly the most influential theory in our century is
that of Max Weber. Weber's theory is built up in layers.
The primary layer is a conception of Europeans as having
been uniquely 'rational' throughout history. Whether or
not this attribute of superior rationality rests, in turn, on
a more basic layer of racial superiority is not made clear.
(On racial influences, see Weber, 1951: 230-32, 379; 1958:
30-31; 1967: 387; 1981: 379). Such a view was indeed dominant in mainstream European thought in Weber's time.
Weber, however, considered non-European Caucasians as
well as non-Caucasians to have inferior rationality. But
he did not offer a clear explanation for the superior rationality of Europeans, nor even a clear definition of 'rationality'. (See Löwith, 1982: 41-52; Freund, 1969. See Weber,
1951: 1-32 for an exhaustive list of the ways in which
Europeans are uniquely rational.) European rationality,
in turn, underlay and explained the unique dynamism of
a great range of European social institutions (Blaut forthcoming). The role of religion was considered crucial,
although it appears that Weber considered different religions to be either more or less rational, hence gave causal
primacy to rationality. Other traits and institutions are
then viewed mainly as products of rational thought (cru-
cially including valuation), sometimes in direct causality,
sometimes via religion (as when Confucianism is blamed
for some negative traits of the Chinese and Christianity
is credited for some positive traits of Europeans: see
Weber, 1951: 226-49), although Weber was neither sim-
plistic nor deterministic, and gave careful attention to economic and even geographic factors as well as the
ideological-level ones. The most important outcomes of
superior European rationality, sometimes expressed

through religion, and modified in ways I have mentioned, are these: urbanization processes in Europe which favour economic development in contrast to those of non-Europe which are not dynamic, however grand they may be in scale; landholding systems in Europe which point toward private property and toward capitalism in contrast to non-European land systems in which the holder is only a temporary occupant, granted land on condition of service; and governmental systems, such as bureaucracy, in Europe, which are efficient, rational, and progressive, unlike non-European systems which are rigid and stagnant. Weber is probably the most important and brilliant modern analyst of social phenomena in general and European society in particular, but his theories about European superiority over other civilizations are unfounded. The 'rationality' which is claimed to underlie other facts is purely a theoretical construct, which Weber defends anecdotally. (Example: 'The typical distrust of the Chinese for one another is confirmed by all observers. It stands in sharp contrast to the trust and honesty of the [Puritans]': Weber, 1951: 232.) Europeans, throughout history, have not displayed more intelligence, virtue, and innovativeness than non-Europeans. If pre-1492 urbanization is fairly compared, epoch for epoch, Europe does not stand out: the Weberian image of medieval European cities as uniquely free, uniquely progressive, etc., is invalid. (See Brenner, 1976; Blaut, 1976; G.S. Hamilton, 1985.) Feudal landholding systems included both service and property-like tenure both in Europe and in non-Europe. The rational political institutions of Europe are results, not causes, of modernization. And so forth. In sum: Weber's views of non-Europe were mainly a codification of typical turn-of-the-century diffusionist prejudices, myths, and half-truths about non-Europeans. They prove no European superiority for pre-modern epochs.

As geographers we are (for our sins) familiar with another kind of argument about the superiority of Europeans, an argument grounded in what seem to be the 'hard' facts

of environment, technology, demography, and the like, in
seeming contrast to ideological-level theories like those of
(typical) Weber. In Ritter's time, the European environment was considered superior because God made it so.
Some historians of more recent times, however, invoke the
environment as an independent material cause.
Northwestern Europe has a climate favouring 'human
energy' and agriculture (Jones, 1981: 7, 47). (This is old-
fashioned environmentalism.) Its soils are uniquely fertile
(Mann, 1988; Hall, 1985). (More environmentalism.) Its
indented coastline, capes and bays, favour commerce.
(Archipelagos, rivers, canals, and unindented coasts are
in no way inferior, nor was land transport 1000 years ago.)
Recent historians also reproduce the old myth about Asian
aridity, deducing therefrom irrigation-based societies,
thus Oriental despotism (nowadays described as a propensity toward the 'imperial' state) and cultural stagnation
(Wittfogel, 1957; Jones, 1981; Hall, 1985; Mann, 1988).
But most farming regions of Asia are not at all arid. And
so on.

It appears that most of the recent arguments positing
and explaining the 'European miracle' have a definite, if
not always clearly stated, logical structure. European
superiority of mind, rationality, is the major independent
and primary cause. Europe's superior environment is the
minor independent cause, invoked by many (perhaps most)
historians but not given very much weight. Each historian then points to one or several or (usually) many
European cultural qualities, at one or or more historical
periods, which are explained, explicitly or implicitly, as
products of European rationality or environment, and then
are asserted to be the effective causes, the motors, which
propelled Europe into a more rapid social evolution than
non-Europe. There are many 'miracle' theories, differing
in the parts of culture chosen as cause and the time-peri-
od and place) chosen as venue. Sometimes the same argu-
ment-structure is used with negative assertions about
non-European cultural qualities. The popular word now is

'blockages'. No longer claiming that non-European societies are absolutely stagnant, and absolutely lacking in
the potential to develop, historians now assert that such-
and-such a cultural feature 'blocked' development in such-
and-such a society. (Perhaps just an improvement in
phrasing.) By way of concluding this brief discussion of
'miracle' theories, I will give a few examples of formula-
tions which have this structure of argument.

Lynn White, Jr. (1962) has put forward the strongest
modern argument that European technology explains
Europe's unique medieval progress. On close inspection,
the argument is not about technology but about rationality: Europeans are uniquely inventive (White, 1968).
Rather magically a number of crucial technological innovations are supposed to have popped up in early-medieval
northern Europe, and then to have propelled that region
into rapid modernization. Three of the most crucial traits
are the heavy plough, the three-field system, and the
horse-collar. The heavy plough is assigned, by White, a
tentative central-European origin in the 6th century, then
diffused quickly throughout northwestern Europe, and
'does much to account for the bursting vitality of the
Carolingian realm' (White, 1962: 54). Adoption of the trait
led to a social revolution in northern Europe. It forced
peasants to learn cooperative endeavor. It was crucial to
the rise of manorialism (p. 44). It produced a profound
change in the 'attitude toward nature' and toward property (p. 56). In fact, the heavy plough definitely was crucial in opening up large regions of heavy, wet soil, thus in
enlarging cultivated acreage. But the heavy plough, with
teams of up to 24 oxen, was in use in northern India before
the time of Christ (Kosambi, 1969; Panikkar, 1959). In
Europe it reflected either diffusion or relatively minor
adaptation of lighter plough-technology, long used in drier
parts of Europe. Moreover, all of the causal arguments
from plough to social change can be reversed: the evolution of feudalism led to an immense demand for more cultivated acreage, and this led to an adaptation of plough

technology such that heavy-soil regions could now be cultivated. The technology is effect, not cause, and Europeans are not displayed as uniquely inventive and thus uniquely progressive. White's arguments concerning the three-field system and the horse-collar deserve roughly the same response (Blaut forthcoming), as do all of the other technological traits discussed by White (1962), most of which either diffused into Europe from elsewhere or were evolved in common among many cultures in many regions. White's explanation for the supposed uniquely inventive character of Europeans is quite Weberian. European inventiveness is attributed basically to 'the Judeo-Christian teleology' and to 'Western Christianity'. The former underlies the European's unique 'faith in perpetual progress' (White, 1968: 85), which becomes a faith in technology. The latter produces 'an Occidental, voluntarist realization of the Christian dogma of man's transcendence of, and rightful mastery over, nature...[There is no] spirit in nature' (p. 90). Nature is tool. But medieval Europeans tended not to believe in progress: God's world was created perfect and entire. This belief is not ancient but modern; White is simply telescoping history. And medieval Europeans did not separate man from nature: they believed in the plenum, the great chain of being, the presence of God in all things. Moreover, Eastern Christianity and non-Christian doctrines have parallels with the Western ones. This is not an explanation.

In the 1980s a number of works appeared which strongly defended the historical superiority of Europe and the basic diffusionist thesis that non-Europe always lagged in history. The most widely-discussed of these works is Eric Jones' book *The European Miracle* (Jones, 1981). Jones, an economic historian, assembles essentially all of the traditional arguments for Europe's historical superiority, including some (like Europe's 'climatic energy') which have been definitively refuted, and adds to these a number of colonial-era myths about the cultural and psychological inability of non-European societies to modernize. Jones' basic arguments are the following:

(1) Europe's environment is superior to Asia's and Africa's.
(2) Europeans are rational, others are not.
(3) As a result of their superior rationality, Europeans control their population, and so accumulate wealth and resources, whereas others do not.

The argument is developed in a series of steps. First, Jones invokes environmentalism to make various spurious claims about the superiority of the European environment, about Asia's aridity and the consequent 'Oriental despotism, 'authoritarianism', 'political infantilism' (p. 10), etc. Next, he states as fact the completely speculative claim that ancient northern European society had qualities favouring progress and population control and so set Europeans on their permanent course of development. The claim is that lack of irrigated agriculture (the root of Oriental despotism) and rustic forest life led to individualism, love of freedom, and aggressiveness, thus a unique psychology, and also to the favouring of the nuclear family. Only speculation leads one from known evidence about settlement patterns to the conclusion that early Europeans had a special partiality toward nuclear families. (Jones confuses settlement, household, and kinship.) Jones simply asserts that the north-European post-Neolithic nuclear family became a permanent (and unique) European trait and permitted Europeans — in contrast to Asians — to avoid the Malthusian curse of overpopulation. (Here he repeats the myth of early modernization theory that nuclear families somehow lead to a 'preference...for goods rather than for children': p. 12.) There is no reason to believe that ancient European cultures had any qualities uniquely favouring historical change: this is merely one of the classic European prejudices.

Jones then proceeds to explain the rise of capitalism. This reflected environmental factors, ancient cultural factors, and also particular medieval outcomes. Jones repeats White's arguments about technological inventiveness. Europe was a uniquely 'inventive society' (p. 227). *Et cetera*. He constructs a theory to the effect that Europe's environmental diversity produced a pattern of separate small states, the embryos of the modern nation-states, whereas Asia's supposedly uniform landscapes favoured (along with irrigation) the imperial form of government. Jones (also see Hall, 1985) claims that empires stifle economic development, although he gives no reason other than the saw about Oriental despotism and the false picture of Asian landscapes (which are as diversified as the European). His basic argument-form is: capitalism and no empire in Europe, no capitalism and empire in Asia, ergo empire blocks capitalism.

The final step is to show that Asia and Africa had no potential whatever for development. Jones calls this 'the comparative method' (p. 153) but it is really just a string of negative statements about Africa and Asia. Africa is disposed of with a few ugly comments. 'In Africa, man adapted himself to nature...felt part of the ecosystem...not above it and superior' (p. 154). Africans did not know the wheel, made no contribution to world civilization. Etcetera. Asians do not have the capacity for logical thought (pp. 161-3). They have a 'servile spirit', a 'love of luxury' (p. 167). There is much thievery, senseless warfare, obscurantism, and general irrationality, particularly in matters of sexual behaviour. ('[In Asia] population was permitted to grow without...deliberate restraint...Seemingly, copulation was preferred above commodities': p. 15.) Jones concludes that such societies could not progress in history. Development 'would have been supermiraculous' (p. 238).

I lack the space to review other recent efforts of this sort to prove that there was a 'European miracle' and to explain it. Brief mention should however be made of certain arguments put forward by John A. Hall (1985, 1988) and Michael Mann (1986, 1988). (See Blaut 1989b.) Both Hall and Mann adopt the major arguments of Weber, White, and Jones, including the aridity-irrigation-despotism formula, then add special arguments of their own. Mann thinks that ancient Europeans acquired a peculiarly democratic, individualistic, progressive culture, with power dispersed widely instead of being concentrated despotically, because, among other things, they adopted (and presumably invented) iron-working in agriculture, iron being widely available to the individual peasant (but we do not know where iron metallurgy was invented and iron-working was adopted rather quickly from China to West Africa). He also posits a teleological tendency of Europeans to march northwestward, clearing marvelously fertile land as they proceed, eventually reaching the sea and, with peculiar venturesomeness, expanding across the world. Like Weber and White, he gives a major role in this march to Western Christianity, claiming that it gave West-Europeans historical advantages over peoples with other religions. Hall prefers to emphasize Europeans' uniquely progressive polities along with Europeans' uniquely rational demographic behaviour ('the relative continence of the European family': Hall, 1985: 131). In India, caste hobbled state development. ('India did not have a political *history*: p. 76. India 'had no sense of brotherhood': Hall, 1988: 28.) In China, empire prevented progress. The Islamic realm was mainly a zone of tribal nomads with a fanatical ideology and only unstable polities. Europe had an implicitly modern ('organic') state from very early. None of this requires comment.

The new 'European miracle' literature exemplified by the works of Jones, Mann, and Hall should be seen in perspective. In recent decades a reaction to Eurocentric history has emerged, a kind of 'Third-Worldist' revisionism, with notable contributions by J. Abu-Lughod, H. Alavi, S. Amin, M. Bernal, A. Cabral, J. Cockcroft, B. Davidson, A.G. Frank, C. Furtado, E. Galeano, I. Habib, C.L.R. James, M. Moreno Fraginals, J. Needham, W. Rodney, E. Said, R.S. Sharma, R. Thapar, I. Wallerstein, E. Williams, and many other European and non-European writers. I sense that Eurocentric historians basically ignored this revisionism for some time, then, in the 1970s, began a vigorous counterattack. Although the revisionists had not yet

focused on pre-1492 European history, it was evident that
the counterattack would have to strengthen the foundation axiom that Europe has been the evolutionary leader
among world civilizations since far back in history, long
before 1492, proving that non-Europe has not contributed
significantly to European or world history, and that non-
Europe's underdevelopment resulted from its own historical failings (stagnation, blocked development), not from
European colonialism. This is the new wave of diffusionist tunnel history.

Landscapes of Even Development

Was Europe more advanced in level or rate of development than Asia and Africa in the late Middle Ages? The
evidence which I will now summarize suggests that this
was not the case. (See Blaut, 1976, 1987b, 1989a.) The
major modes of production which were widespread in
Europe were also widespread in the other continents. The
cultural attributes which would tend to be involved in cultural evolution out of feudalism and toward capitalism and
modernity were present in the main social formations of
Asia and Africa as well as Europe in 1492. I do not think
it is necessary to insist upon a definite theory, Marxist or
non-Marxist, as to how and why feudalism decayed and
capitalism (and modernity) arose, in order to defend the
thesis that the process, viewed at the continental scale,
was going on *evenly*, not *unevenly*, across the medieval Old
World. The parts of culture which seem to me to be central to the process, namely, forms and relations of production, urbanization, large-scale commerce and
commodity movement, and the ideas and social structures
associated with economic and technological development,
all seem to have been present in many societies across the
hemisphere. Moreover, there seems to have been a single
intercommunicating social network, in which criss-cross
diffusion spread each new development widely across the
hemisphere, leading to even, instead of uneven development. I have argued this thesis elsewhere, and will very

briefly summarize it here.

Perhaps half of the agriculturally settled portions of Africa, Asia, and Europe had landlord-dominated societies in which surplus was extracted from peasants, some of whom (in all three continents) were serfs, others free tenants. The mode of production was feudal (see Blaut, 1976). The European version of this mode of production had no special characteristics which would suggest more rapid transformation into another mode of production. To give a few examples: the European manorial system, sometimes considered a milestone on the road to private property and production, had parallels in China and India and doubtless elsewhere (including sub-Saharan Africa), and in any case the integrated demesne had largely disappeared in Western Europe by the 13th century. (Choudhary, 1974; Elvin, 1973; Fei, 1953; Gopal, 1963; Isichei, 1983; Kea, 1882; Liceria, 1974; Mahalingam, 1951; Sharma, 1965; A. Smith, 1971; Watson, 1983; Tung, 1965; Yadava, 1974). Serfdom tended to decline in Europe from the 14th century, but medieval-period tenancy based on untied peasants was widespread in South China and other places, and was sometimes (as in Fukien) associated with commercial production of industrial products (Rawski, 1972). The European feudal estate was not closer to genuine cumulable private property (and capital) than were estates in many other areas, including China and part of India. (The old generalization, popularized by Weber, that Asian land ownership was based on service tenure while the European was heritable private property is simply historically untrue. Service estates tended to evolve with time into privately owned estates, service tenure was legally characteristic of feudal Europe as much as most other regions, and rotation of estates tended to reflect special situations of politico-military instability. See Chandra, 1981; Chicherov, 1976; Elvin, 1973; Gopal, 1963; Mahalingam, 1951; Sharma, 1965; Thapar, 1982.) The cash tenancy which replaced serfdom in some parts of Western Europe in the 14th and 15th century had close parallels in other continents (Alavi, 1982; Chandra, 1981; Kea, 1982; Rawski, 1972; Yadava, 1966). And so on.

Was feudalism collapsing in Europe more rapidly than elsewhere? Two common measures used to judge this point are peasant unrest and urbanization (implicitly rural-urban migration). Peasant revolts seem to have been widespread and intense in other continents (Parsons, 1970; Harrison, 1968). The movement to towns was if anything less intense in Europe in the later Middle Ages than elsewhere, since urban population still represented a much lower percent of total populations than in many non-European regions (perhaps including sub-Saharan Africa: see Niane 1984), lower even in classical feudal countries like France than in the Mediterranean countries of Europe. Doubtless, feudalism was collapsing or crumbling, but this was happening at a relatively slow rate and was happening also elsewhere in the hemisphere (Alavi, 1982; Chandra, 1981; Chicherov, 1976; Elvin, 1973; Kea, 1982).

I suspect that Marx and Engels were right in seeing the decline of the feudal mode of production and the rise of capitalism as a dual process involving crisis in rural feudal class relations and rise of towns and their non-feudal class processes. But urbanization and the development of urban economies was fully as advanced in parts of Africa and Asia as it was in the most advanced parts of Europe. This applies to commerce, to the rise of a bourgeoisie and a working class, to the attaining of sufficient autonomy to allow the development of legal and political systems appropriate to capitalism. There is of course the theory that European cities were somehow free while Asian cities were under the tight control of the surrounding polity. The principal basis for this view is the ideology of diffusionism which imagines that everything important in early Europe was imbued with freedom while everything important in Asia (not to mention Africa) was ground under 'Oriental despotism' until the Europeans came and brought freedom. (Montesquieu and

Quesnay believed this. Marx believed it. Weber believed it. Many believe it today.) The so-called 'free cities' of central Europe were hardly the norm and were not, in most cases, crucial for the rise of capitalism. The partial autonomy of many mercantile-maritime port cities of Europe, from Italy to the North Sea, was of course a reality, and usually reflected either the dominance by the city of a relatively small polity (often a city-state) or the gradual accommodation of feudal states to their urban sectors, allowing the latter considerable autonomy because of considerations of profit or power. But all of this held true also in many cities of Africa and Asia. Small mercantile-maritime cities and city-states dotted the coasts of the Indian Ocean and the South China Seas like pearls on a string (Das Gupta, 1967; Maleiev, 1984; Simkin, 1968). Within large states, mutual accommodation between city and polity was very common (as in Mughal India). And in general, it appears that all of the progressive characteristics of late-medieval urbanization in Europe were found at the same time in other parts of the hemisphere.

The Hemisphere-Wide Transition

Just before 1492 a slow transition toward capitalism was taking place in many regions of Asia, Africa, and Europe. On all three continents there were centers of incipient capitalism, protocapitalism, most of them highly urbanized, and most of them seaports. These protocapitalist centers, primarily urban but often with large hinterlands of commercialized agriculture (Das Gupta, 1967; Naqvi, 1968; Nicholas, 1967-68; Rawski, 1973), bore various relationships to the feudal landscapes against which they abutted. Some were independent city-states. Some were themselves small (and unusual) feudal states. Some were wholly contained within larger feudal states but had sufficient autonomy in matters relating to capitalist enterprise that the feudal overlordship did not serious cramp their style.

The mercantile-maritime, protocapitalist centers of the

Eastern Hemisphere were connected tightly with one another in networks — ultimately a single network — along which flowed material things, people, and ideas (Blaut, 1976; Abu-Lughod, 1989). The links had been forged over many centuries: some were in place even in the days when China traded with Rome. By 1492, these centers were so closely interlinked that the growth and prosperity of each of them was highly dependent on that of many others; ultimately, on all of them. By 1492, the centers had become, in many ways, little capitalist societies. They were seats of production as well as commodity movement. They held distinct populations of workers and bourgeoisie (or proto-bourgeoisie), and the worker-capitalist relation was very likely the dominant class relation. They had already developed most of the institutions that we find present in capitalist society at the time of the bourgeois revolution or revolutions of the 17th century. They cannot be compared to industrial capitalist societies of the 19th century, but then we have to remember that capitalism in Europe went through a long pre-industrial phase, and the descriptions of industrial capitalism after, say, 1800 cannot properly be used to characterize the pre-industrial phase. The centers of 1492 were primarily engaged in moving commodities produced in the surrounding feudal societies, but this should not mislead us into thinking of them either as component parts of those societies or as being somehow feudal themselves, on the model of the merchant communities which flourished everywhere during the feudal period.

The small centers as well as the large were emitting and receiving commodities, technologies, ideas of all sorts, people, in a continuous criss-crossing of diffusions (Blaut, 1987a). It is not difficult to understand that, in spite of their cultural differences, their distances from one another, their different political characteristics, their different sizes, they were sharing a common process: the gradual rise of capitalism within late feudal society. Thus it is not at all unreasonable to think of the landscape of rising cap-

italism as an even one, stretching from Europe to Africa
and Asia in spots and nodes, but everywhere at the same
level of development.

Explaining Fourteen Ninety-Two

In 1492, as have seen, capitalism was slowly emerging
and feudalism declining in many parts of Asia, Africa, and
Europe. In that year there would have been no reason
whatever to predict that capitalism would triumph in
Europe, and would triumph only two centuries later. By
'the triumph of capitalism' I mean the rise of a bourgeoisie
to unquestioned political power: the bourgeois revolutions.
This was really a revolutionary epoch, occurring throughout many European countries at varying rates, but I will
follow convention in dating it symbolically to 1688, the
year of England's 'Glorious Revolution'. It should be
emphasized that the capitalism which triumphed was not
industrial capitalism. How this pre-industrial capitalism
should be conceptualized is a difficult question because it
is something much larger than the 'merchant capital' of
medieval times. But the industrial revolution did not really begin until the end of the 18th century, and those who
conceptualize the industrial revolution as simply a continuation of the bourgeois revolution are neglecting a large
block of history, inside and outside of Europe.

The explanation for the rise of capitalism to political
power in Europe between 1492 and 1688 requires an
understanding of (1) the reasons why Europeans, not
Africans and Asians, reached and conquered America, (2)
the reasons why the conquest was successful, and (3) the
direct and indirect effects of the 16th-century plunder of
American resources and exploitation of American workers
on the transformation of Europe, and of 17th-century colonial and semi-colonial European enterprise in America,
Africa, and Asia on the further transformation of Europe
and eventually the political triumph of capitalism in the

bourgeois revolution. We will summarize each of these processes in turn.

Why America Was Conquered by Europeans and Not by Africans or Asians

One of the core myths of Eurocentric diffusionism concerns the discovery of America. Typically it goes something like this: Europeans, being more progressive, venturesome, achievement-oriented, and modern than Africans and Asians in the late Middle Ages, and with superior technology as well as a more advanced economy, went forth to explore and conquer the world. And so they set sail down the African coast in the middle of the 15th century and out across the Atlantic to America in 1492. This myth is crucial for diffusionist ideology for two reasons: it explains the modern expansion of Europe in terms of internal, immanent forces, and it permits one to acknowledge that the conquest and its aftermath (Mexican mines, West Indian plantations, North American settler colonies, etc.) had significance for European history without at the same time requiring one to give any credit in that process to non-Europeans.

In reality, the Europeans were doing what everyone else was doing across the hemisphere-wide network of proto-capitalist, mercantile-maritime centers, and Europeans had no special qualities or advantages, no peculiar venturesomeness, no peculiarly advanced maritime technology, or suchlike. What they did have was opportunity: a matter of locational advantage in the broad sense of accessibility. The point deserves to be put very strongly. If the Western Hemisphere had been more accessible, say, to South Indian centers than to European centers, then very likely India would have become the home of capitalism, the site of the bourgeois revolution, and the ruler of the world.

In the late Middle Ages, long-distance oceanic voyaging was being undertaken by mercantile-maritime communities everywhere. In the 15th century, Africans were

sailing to India, Indians to Africa, Arabs to China, Chinese
to Africa, and so on (Chaudhuri, 1985; Simkin, 1968).
Much of this voyaging was across open ocean and much of
it involved exploration. Two non-European examples are
well-known: Cheng Ho's voyages to India and Africa
between 1417 and 1433, and an Indian voyage around the
Cape of Good Hope and apparently some 2000 miles westward into the Atlantic in c.1420 (Filesi, 1972; Ma Huan,,
1970; Panikkar, 1959). In this period, the radii of travel
were becoming longer, as a function of the general evolution of protocapitalism, the expansion of trade, and the
development of maritime technology. Maritime technology differed from region to region but no one region could
be considered to have superiority in any sense implying
evolutionary advantage (Lewis, 1973; Needham, 1971, vol.
4, part 3). (There is a widely held but mistaken belief that
Chinese imperial policy prevented merchants from engag-
ing in seaborne trade during the late 15th and early 16th
centuries. On this matter see Purcell, 1965; So, 1975;
Wiethoff, 1963. I discuss the issue in Blaut, 1976, note 17.)
Certainly the growth of Europe's commercial economy led
to the Portuguese and Spanish voyages of discovery. But
the essence of the process was a matter of catching up with
Asian and African protocapitalist communities by
European communities which were at the margin of the
system and were emerging from a period of downturn relative to other parts of the system. Iberian Christian states
were in conflict with Maghreb states and European merchant communities were having commercial difficulties
both there and in the eastern Mediterranean. The opening of a sea-route to West African gold mining regions,
along a sailing route known since antiquity and using maritime technology known to non-Europeans as well as
Europeans, was obvious strategy. By the late 15th century the radii of travel had lengthened so that a sea route
to India was found to be feasible (with piloting help from
African and Indian sailors). The leap across the Atlantic
in 1492 was certainly one of the great adventures of human

history, but it has to be seen in a context of shared technological and geographical knowledge, high potential for
commercial success, and other factors which place it, in a
hemispheric perspective, as something that could have
been undertaken by non-Europeans just as easily as by
Europeans.

Europeans had one advantage. America was vastly
more accessible from Iberian ports than from any extra-
European mercantile-maritime centers which had the
capacity for long-distance sea voyages. Accessibility was
in part a matter of sailing distance. Sofala was some 3000
miles farther than the Canary Islands (Columbus' jump-
ing-off point) and more than 4000 miles farther from any
densely populated coast with attractive possibilities for
trade or plunder. The distance from China to America's
northwest coast was even greater, and greater still to the
rich societies of Mexico. To all of this we must add the
sailing conditions on these various routes. Sailing from the
Indian Ocean into the Atlantic one sails against prevailing winds. The North Pacific is somewhat stormy and
winds are not reliable. From the Canaries to the West
Indies, on the other hand, there blow the trade winds, and
the return voyage is made northward into the westerlies.
Obviously an explorer does not have this information at
hand at the time of the voyage into unknown seas
(although the extent of the geographical knowledge pos-
sessed by Atlantic fishing communities in the 15th century remains an unanswered and intriguing question, and
the navigational strategies employed customarily by
Iberian sailors going to and from the Atlantic islands
would have been similar to those employed by Columbus
in crossing the Atlantic: a matter of utilizing the easter-
lies outward and westerlies homeward). The point here is
a matter of probabilities. Overall, it is vastly more probable that an Iberian ship would effect a passage to America
than would an African or Asian ship in the late 15th century, and, even if such a voyage were made, it is vastly
more probable that Columbus' landfall in the West Indies

would initiate historical consequences than would have been the case for an African ship reaching Brazil or a Chinese ship reaching California.

Is this environmentalism? There is no more environmentalism here than there is in, say, some statement about the effect of oilfields on societies of the Middle East. I am asserting only the environmental conditions which support and hinder long-distance oceanic travel. In any case, if the choice were between an environmentalistic explanation and one that claimed fundamental superiority of one group over all others, as Eurocentric diffusionism does, would we not settle for environmentalism?

Before we leave this topic, there remain two important questions. First, why did not West Africans discover America since they were even closer to it than the Iberians were? The answer seems to be that mercantile, protocapitalist centers in West and Central Africa were not oriented to commerce by sea (as were those of East Africa). The great long-distance trade routes led across the Sudan to the Nile and the Middle East, across the Sahara to the Maghreb and the Mediterranean, etc. Sea trade existed all along the western coast, but apparently it was not important, given that civilizations were mainly inland and trading partners lay northward and eastward (see Devisse and Labib, 1984). Second, why did not the trading cities of the Maghreb discover America? This region (as Ibn Khaldun noted not long before) was in a political and commercial slump. In 1492 it was under pressure from the Iberians and the Turks. Just at that historical conjuncture, this region lacked a capacity for major long-distance oceanic voyaging.

Why the Conquest Was Successful

America became significant in the rise of Europe, and the rise of capitalism, soon after the first contact in 1492. Immediately a process began, and explosively enlarged, involving the destruction of American states and civilizations, the plunder of precious metals, the exploitation of labour, and the occupation of American lands by Europeans. If we are to understand the impact of all of this on Europe (and capitalism), we have to understand how it occurred and why it happened so quickly; why, in a word, the conquest was successful.

There is a second crucial reason why we need to understand the causality of the conquest. A non-diffusionist history starts all causal arguments with the working hypothesis that Europeans were not superior to non-Europeans. This leads first to a recognition that Europeans in 1492 had no special advantage over Asians and Africans, ideological, social, or material. But it demands that we make the same working hypothesis about Western Hemisphere communities. Why, then, did Europeans discover America instead of Americans discovering Europe (or Africa, or Asia)? And why, after the first contact, did Europeans conquer the American civilizations instead of being defeated and driven from America's shores? The working hypothesis of cultural uniformitarianism (Blaut, 1987a) here confronts the diffusionist tendency to dismiss the peoples of America as primitive and in any case irrelevant.

There were several immediate reasons why American civilizations succumbed, but one of these reasons is of paramount importance and may perhaps be a sufficient cause in and of itself. This is the massive depopulation caused by the pandemics of Eastern Hemisphere disease introduced to the Americas by Europeans (Crosby, 1972; Denevan, 1976). A second factor was the considerable advantage which Europeans had in military technology, but this advantage has to be kept in perspective. The technological gap was not so great that it could by itself bring military victory — after the initial battles — against American armies which were much larger and would sooner or later have adopted the enemy's technology. None of this happened because the Americans were dying in epidemics, apparently even before the battles were joined. Probably 90% of the population of highland Mexico succumbed during the 16th century; the majority of deaths occurred early enough to assist the political conquest (Borah and Cook, 1972). Parallel processes took place in other parts of the hemisphere, especially where there were major concentrations of population, these in most cases being areas of state organization and high civilization. Perhaps three-quarters of the entire population of the Americas was wiped out during that century. Millions died in battle with the Spaniards and Portuguese and in slave-labour centers such as the mines of Mexico and Peru, but much greater numbers died in epidemics, and this was the reason why organized resistance to the conquest was rapidly overcome in most (not all) areas.

Both the lower level of military technology among Western Hemisphere peoples and the susceptibility of American populations to Eastern Hemisphere diseases can be explained in fairly straightforward cultural-evolutionary terms, although evidence bearing on the matter is generally indirect. The Western Hemisphere was not occupied by humans until very late in the Paleolithic period: probably not before 30,000 B.P. The immigrants did not possess agriculture. The earliest migrations preceded the agricultural revolution in the Eastern Hemisphere; in addition, the source area for the migrations, northeastern Siberia, is generally too cold for agriculture, even for present-day agriculture, and we would not expect to find that these cultures were experimenting with incipient agriculture 20,000 years or so ago although some low-latitude cultures were doing so. Migrants to America were paleolithic hunters, gatherers, fishers, and shellfishers. They came in small numbers and spread throughout both North and South America. Only after some millennia had passed was the stock of resources for hunting, fishing, gathering, and shellfishing under any significant pressure from humans: one assumes that population growth was slow but — this is of course speculative — that population growth eventually did reach the point where conditions were favourable to an agricultural revolution. In the

Eastern Hemisphere the agricultural revolution seems to have occurred (as a qualitative change) roughly 10-12,000 years ago. In the Western Hemisphere that point may have been reached perhaps 4,000 years later. Thereafter, cultural evolution in the Western Hemisphere proceeded along lines somewhat parallel to those of Eastern Hemisphere evolution: the development of agricultural societies, of classes, of ceremonial centers, cities, feudal class structures, and incipient merchant capitalism. It seems that the Western Hemisphere societies were closing the gap. But in 1492, military technology in the most advanced and powerful states was still well behind that of Eastern Hemisphere states. Hence the superiority of Cortés's armies over Moctezuma's and Pizarro's over the Inca's. (When Cortés first arrived at Tenochtitlán the Aztecs were already dying in great numbers from European diseases which, apparently, had been carried by American traders from Cuba to Mexico. Likewise, the Incas were succumbing to these diseases before Pizarro arrived. See Crosby, 1972.)

The susceptibility of American populations to Eastern Hemisphere diseases, and the consequent devastation of American settlements, collapse of states, and defeat and subjugation by the Europeans, is explained within the same general model. Small populations entered the Americas and probably bore with them only a small subset of the diseases which existed in the Eastern Hemisphere at the time of their departure. They came, in addition, from a rather isolated, thinly populated part of the hemisphere, and a part which, having a cold climate, would have lacked some diseases characteristic of warm regions. Perhaps more important is the history of the diseases themselves. Many diseases seem to have originated or become epidemiologically significant during or after the agricultural revolution, and to have ecological connections to agriculture, land-management, and settlement changes associated with agricultural and later urbanized communities. In the Eastern Hemisphere humanity entered these ecological situations after the initial migrations to the Western Hemisphere, hence the migrants would not have carried with them these diseases. Later migrants may have done so (although this is again unlikely because they came from a cold and isolated part of Asia). But we can assume that the sparse settlement, the hunting-gathering-fishing-shellfishing way of life, and the absence of agricultural settlements and urbanization in the Americas during many millennia, would have caused a disappearance of some of the Eastern Hemisphere diseases which had been carried across to America by migrants. After a time, the American populations would have lost their physiological immunities to diseases no longer present in these populations, and they would of course lack immunities to diseases never before encountered. It is known, in this regard, that utter devastation was produced in the Americas from diseases to which Eastern Hemisphere populations had such high levels of immunity that they experienced some of these diseases as minor maladies only (Crosby, 1972; Denevan, 1976: 5; Wachtel, 1984).

Hence there is no need to take seriously any longer the various myths which explain the defeat of the Americans in terms of imputed irrationality or superstitiousness or any of the other classical, often racist, myths about American civilizations in 1492 (such as the myth that Mexicans imagined Cortés to be a god). The relatively minor difference in technology between the two communities, and the impact of Eastern Hemisphere diseases upon Western Hemisphere communities, can be explained in terms of the settlement history of the Western Hemisphere and its consequences.

After Fourteen Ninety-Two
Europe in Fourteen Ninety-Two

In 1492, European society was rather sluggishly moving out of feudalism and toward capitalism. Nothing in the landscape would suggest that a revolutionary transformation was imminent, or even suggest that the social and economic changes taking place were very rapid. The growth of the English woolen trade in the 15th century was not (as it is often depicted) a sign of revolutionary economic change: it was complemented by a decline in competing woolen industries elsewhere in Europe (Miskimin, 1969). Rural growth in this century reflected mainly population recovery (in some areas) after the great plagues of the preceding century, and the commercialization of agriculture that was then taking place had been doing so for some time (Abel, 1980). Towns were growing, but only slowly, and the urban population was still a very small fraction of total population (except in Italy and the Low Countries), and smaller than it was in many non-European areas (de Vries, 1984; Appadorai, 1936; Habib, 1963). There were strong signs even of economic contraction instead of growth (Lopez and Miskimin, 1961-62; C. T. Smith, 1967). For Hodgett (1972: 212), the 200 year period 1320-1520 was 'a period of downturn in the [European] economy as a whole'. The Italian Renaissance, in economic terms, did not raise the Italian centers above the level of many non-European centers, and it was not at all a technological revolution (Lopez, 1953; Thorndyke, 1943). All of this needs to be said by way of setting the stage. Before 1492 there was slow growth in Europe, perhaps even a down-turn, and certainly no revolution.

Within a few decades after 1492, the rate of growth and change speeded up dramatically, and Europe entered a period of rapid development. There is no dispute about this fact, which is seen in the known statistics relating to the

16th-century price revolution, urban growth, and much more beside (Braudel, 1967; de Vries, 1984; Fisher, 1989). What is disputable is the causal connection between these explosive changes and the beginnings of economic exploitation in America (and, significant but secondary, in Africa and Asia). There is agreement that the effect was profound. But did it truly generate a qualitative transformation in Europe's economy? Or did it merely modify a process already well underway? This question cannot be answered unless we break out of the European historical tunnel and look at what was going on in the Americas, Asia, and Africa between 1492 and 1688, the symbolic date for Europe's bourgeois revolution.

Colonialism and Capitalism in the Sixteenth and Seventeenth Centuries

Enterprise in the Americas was from the start a matter of capital accumulation: of profit. No matter if some feudal traits were incorporated in legal and land-granting systems in the Americas, and if the Iberian governments took a substantial share of the profits. The goal of all European groups involved in the enterprise was to make money. The leading group, almost everywhere, was the European protocapitalist class, not only merchants but also industrialists and profit-oriented landlords, not only Iberian but also Italian, Dutch, English, French, German, Austrian, and so on. This class community took the profit from colonial enterprise and invested part of it in Europe, buying land and developing commercial agriculture, developing industries (like shipbuilding, sugar refining, etc.) associated with the growing colonial enterprise, developing profitable businesses in spheres of activity which served the growing European economy, building urban structures, and the like. Part of the profit was ploughed back into other colonial risk enterprise, in America and in the new trading enterprises in southern Asia, Africa, and the Levant. The most subtle aspect of the process was the simple increase in purchases of all sorts by merchants in all markets, European and extra-European, growing out of the fact that these merchants now had incredible amounts of precious metals or metal-based money at their command and could offer previously unheard-of prices. Perhaps half of the gold and silver brought back from the Americas in the 16th century was contraband, hence available directly for this kind of enterprise, but the remainder, after passing through the great customs-houses, quickly entered circulation as the Iberians paid out gold and silver for goods and services.

Colonial enterprise in the 16th century produced capital in a number of ways. One was gold and silver mining. A second was plantation agriculture, principally in Brazil. A third was the trade with Asia in spices, cloth, and much more. A fourth element was the profit returned to European houses from a variety of productive and commercial enterprises in the Americas, including profit on production for local use in Mexico, Peru, etc., profit on sale of goods imported from Europe, profit on many secondary exports from the Americas (leather, dyestuffs, etc.), profit on land sales in the Americas, profit returned to Europe by families and corporations holding land-grants in Mexico and other areas. A fifth was slaving. Notice that most of this is normal capital accumulation; little of it is the mysterious thing called 'primitive accumulation'. (Marxists need to notice that surplus value from wage labour, not to mention forced labour, was involved in all of this, and that much of it was value from production, not simply from trade.) Accumulation from these sources was massive.

Precious Metals. We notice first the export of gold and silver from the Western Hemisphere and its insertion within the circuits of an Old World hemispheric market economy in which gold and silver already provide the common measure of value, directly or indirectly, in almost all markets. The flow of precious metals began immediately after the discovery of America, and by 1640 at least 180 tons of gold and 17,000 tons of silver are known to have reached Europe (E.J. Hamilton, 1934; Brading and Cross, 1972; Chaunu and Chaunu, 1956) — the real figures must be double or triple these amounts, since records were poor for some areas and periods and since contraband was immensely important (Céspedes, 1974; Cross, 1983; McAlister, 1984). Additional quantities of gold came from colonial activities in West and East Africa (Magalhães-Godinho, 1969). In the period 1561-1580 about 85% of the entire world's production of silver came from the Americas. The simple quantity of gold and silver in circulation in the Eastern Hemisphere economy as a whole was profoundly affected: hemispheric silver stock may have been tripled and gold stock increased by 20% during the course of the 16th century as a result of American bullion (Vicens Vives, 1969: 323), and the fact that much of the pre-existing stock must have been frozen in uses not permitting direct or indirect conversion to money suggests to me that American bullion may have as much as doubled the gold and silver base of money supply for the Eastern Hemisphere as a whole. (In Europe, the circulation of metal coins increased eight- or ten-fold in the course of the century: Vilar, 1976: 77.) This process must be seen in perspective: it is money flowing constantly and in massive amounts through Europe and from Europe to Asia and Africa (Atwell, 1982; Hasan, 1969), constantly replenished at the entry points (Seville, Antwerp, Genoa, etc.) with more American supplies, and constantly permitting those who hold it to offer better prices for all goods, as well as labour and land, in all markets, than anyone else had ever been able to offer in prior times.

The importance of these flows of gold and silver is generally underestimated, mainly for three reasons (apart from implicit diffusionism). First, the process is seen somehow as purely primitive accumulation. But the metals were mined by workers and transported by workers, the enterprise overall involved risk capital and all of the other familiar traits of the sorts of protocapitalist productive enterprises which were characteristic of that time (that it was partly state-controlled does not alter this argument, nor does the fact that some of the labour was unfree), and very major economic and social systems were built around the mines themselves in Mexico, Peru, and other parts of America. Secondly, the argument that precious metal flows significantly affected the European economy is dismissed as monetarism. The error in this charge is a failure to see the 16th-century economy in a geographical and social context (and imputing to it the liquidity of exchange and the relative lack of spatial friction which characterizes the capitalist economy of our own time: see Fisher, 1989). Two facts here are basic. On the one hand, the possession of precious metals was highly localized in space. European merchants, as a community, obtained it and set it in motion outward, toward rural Europe and toward markets outside of Europe. On the other hand, the supply of precious metals was essentially continuous, so that the advantage held by European protocapitalists in terms of prices they could offer for commodities, labour, and land was persistently higher than the prices which competitors anywhere could offer. So the protocapitalist community very steadily undermined the competition in markets across the Eastern Hemisphere, within Europe and without, eventually gaining control of most international seaborne trade in most of the mercantile-maritime centers from Sofala to Calicut to Malacca. The penetration of these markets, the acquisition of trading bases, and the control of a few small but important producing areas (like the Moluccas), was not a matter of European rationality or venturesomeness, but rather reflected the availability to Europeans of American gold and silver, transshipped through Lisbon, Acapulco, etc. A third sort of doubt about the importance of American gold and silver is associated with the critique of E.J. Hamilton's classic theory that the precious metal supply produced an imbalance between factors of production in the European economy, produced thereby a windfall of profits, and thus in effect destabilized the economy and moved it toward capitalism

(Hamilton, 1929). Hamilton was one of the few economic historians to perceive that American gold and silver was a crucial, central cause of change in Europe, although he was partly wrong about the mechanisms which brought about this change. The metals did not transform the economy in a direct way. Rather, they enriched the protocapitalist class and thereby gave it the power to immensely accelerate the transformation which was already underway — not only in Europe — toward capitalism as a political and social system, and to prevent non-European capitalists from sharing in the process. American bullion hastened the rise of capitalism and was crucial in the process by which it became centrated in Europe.

Plantations. The impact of the slave plantation system on Europe's economy was felt mainly in the 17th century and thereafter. But part of the general undervaluing of the significance of early colonialism is a tendency not to notice that the plantation was of immense importance even in the 16th century. Moreover, the early history of the Atlantic sugar plantation economy gives a revealing picture of the way in which the protocapitalist colonial economy was eroding the feudal economy. Sugar planting was not a new enterprise, sugar (contrary to myth) was not a rare commodity, and (also contrary to myth) sugar planting was not an insignificant economic curiosity at the fringe of capitalist development. Commercial and feudal cane sugar production was found throughout the Mediterranean in the 15th century (Galloway, 1989; Deerr, 1949-50); if cane sugar was not an important commodity in northern Europe this was because of its price, as against that of sweeteners like honey. Europeans first moved the commercial plantation system out into the newly-settled Atlantic islands from Madeira to São Tomé and then vastly expanded production in the Americas. But throughout the 16th century the new plantations merely *supplanted* the older Mediterranean sugar-producing regions; total production for the Europe-Mediterranean market did not rise until later (Deerr, 1949-50, vol. 1). This was capitalist production displacing feudal production, using the twin advantages of colonialism: empty land and cheap labour. No other industry was as significant as the plantation system for the rise of capitalism before the 19th century.

In 1600 Brazil exported about 30,000 tons of sugar with a gross sale value of £2,000,000 (Simonsen, 1944; Furtado, 1963). This is about double the total value of all exports from England to all of the world in that year (Minchinton, 1969). It will be recalled that British exports in that period, principally of wool, are sometimes considered paradigmatic for the 'awakening', indeed the 'rise', of early-modern Europe. Also in 1600, per capita earnings from sugar in Brazil, for all of the population other than Indians, was about equal to per capita income in Britain later in that century (Edel, 1969). The rate of accumulation in the Brazilian plantation industry was so high at the end of the 16th century that it was able to generate enough capital to finance a doubling of its capacity every two years (Furtado, 1963). Early in the 17th century, the Dutch protocapitalist community (which was heavily involved in the Brazilian sugar enterprise), estimated that annual profit rates in the industry were 56%, totalling nearly £1,000,000. The rate of profit was higher still at the close of the 16th century, when production costs, including the cost of purchasing slaves, amounted to only one-fifth of income from sugar sales (Furtado, 1963). These statistics should be seen against the background of an industry which was not responding to some novel demand for some novel product in an already-rising Europe, but was merely (in essence) undercutting the precapitalist Mediterranean sugar producers of Spain, Italy, Egypt, etc.

Sugar is of course the centerpiece of the plantation system down to the late 18th century. But other kinds of colonial production, mainly but not only agricultural, and fully as close to capitalism as was the Brazilian plantation system, were of some significance even before the end of the

16th century. There was for instance some direct production of spices in the Moluccas and some European involvement with Indian merchant capitalists in the organization of South Indian pepper production (Das Gupta, 1967; Raychaudhuri, 1962). Dyes, tobacco, and other commercially valuable products were flowing from America to Europe. A very large agricultural economy existed in parts of America supplying food, fiber, leather, etc., to the mining and other settlements. Immediately after 1492 (or before?) West-European fishermen and whalers developed an immense industry in Newfoundland and elsewhere on the North American coast.

To all of this must be added the profits from other colonial and semi-colonial activities in the Eastern Hemisphere. The slave trade was highly profitable even in the 16th century. European merchant capitalists of all nations profited greatly from the Lisbon trade with Asia and East Africa in textiles and particularly spices (the Asian spices carried by the Portuguese and sold mainly through Antwerp did not replace the traditional Mediterranean flow but rather added to it, hence providing a novel and important source of accumulation). There was, in addition, considerable profit from the within-Asia trade resulting from the domination of long-distance oceanic trade in East Africa, India, and Southeast Asia by Portugal (with participation also by Spain and later Holland). Broadly speaking, however, accumulation deriving from Western-Hemisphere colonial activities far outweighed that from Eastern activities, colonial and semi-colonial, in the 16th century. Overall, both the quantitative significance, in that century, of production and trade in colonial and semi-colonial areas and the immense profitability of the enterprise, that is, the rapid capital accumulation which it fostered directly and (in Europe) indirectly, add up to a significant vector force, easily able to initiate the process of transformation in Europe.

Effects. There seem to be two particularly good ways

to assess the real significance for the rise of capitalism of 16th century colonial production in America and some other areas along with trading, piracy, and the like, in Asia and Africa. One way is to trace the direct and indirect effects of colonialism on European society, looking for movements of goods and capital, tracing labour flows into industries and regions stimulated or created by colonial enterprise, looking at the way urbanization flourished in those cities which were engaged in colonial (and more generally extra-European) enterprise or were closely connected to it, and the like. This process overall would then be examined in relation to the totality of changes which were taking place in Europe in that century, to determine whether, in Europe itself, changes clearly resulting from the direct and indirect impact of extra-European activities were the prime movers for economic and social change. This task still remains undone. The second way is to attempt to arrive at a global calculation of the amount of labour (free and unfree) that was employed in European enterprises in America, Africa, and Asia, along with the amount of labour in Europe itself which was employed in activities derived from extra-European enterprise, and then to look at these quantities in relation to the total labour market in Europe for economic activities that were connected to the rise of capitalism. This task has not been done either; indeed, as far as I know little research has been done on 16th-century labour forces and labour markets in American settlements or indeed in Europe. So the proposition which I am arguing here, concerning the significance of 16th century colonialism (and related extra-European activities) for the rise of capitalism in Europe, perhaps cannot be tested as yet.

Still, there are very suggestive indications. Some of these have been mentioned already: matters of assessing the quantities and values of colonial exports to Europe. We can also speculate about labour. One approach is through population. The population of Spain and Portugal in the mid-16th century may have been about nine million (De

Vries, 1984). Estimates of 16th-century populations for the Americas vary widely and there is much controversy about population levels and rates of decline (see Denevan, 1976), but for the present, highly speculative, and essentially methodological, argument, we can ignore the controversies and play with global estimates. The population of Mexico at midcentury may have been around six million, a population that was undergoing continuous decline from its pre-conquest level of perhaps 30 million down to one-tenth of that figure (or perhaps less) in 1600 (Borah and Cook, 1972: 89). Populations in the Andean regions involved in mineral and textile production for the Spaniards may (speculating) have totalled five million in the late 16th century. Perhaps we can add an additional two million for the population of other parts of Ibero-America which were within regions of European control and presumably involved, more or less, in the European-dominated economy. Let us, then, use a ball-park estimate of 13 million for the American population that was potentially yielding surplus value to Europeans in the mid-to-late 16th century. The population seems larger than Iberia's. Granted, the comparison should be made with a larger part of Europe, certainly including the Low Countries, which were intimately involved in the exploitation of America (and Asia) at this period, along with parts of Italy and other countries. Assume then a relevant population of 20 million for Europe as against 13 million for America. I see no good reason to argue that the European populations were more centrally involved in the rise of capitalism than the American populations — that is, the 13 million people who we assume were in European dominated regions. It is likely that the proportion of the American population which was engaged in labour for Europeans, as wage work, as forced labour including slave labour, and as the labour of farmers delivering goods as tribute or rent in kind, was no lower than the proportion of Iberian people engaged in labour for commercialized sectors of the Spanish and Portuguese economy. The level of exploitation for Indian labour must have been much higher than that for Iberian labour because portions of the Indian labour force were worked literally to death in this period (Newsom, 1985) — depopulation was due in part to forced labour — and so the capital generated by each worker was very probably higher than that generated by a European worker. (We need to remind ourselves again that we are dealing with a pre-industrial, basically medieval economy in Europe. Workers there did not have higher productivity due to larger capital-labour ratios or higher technology.) We must add next the fact that the capital accumulated from the labour of Americans went directly to the economic sectors in Europe which were building capitalism, whereas most workers and peasants in Europe were still connected to basically medieval sectors of the economy. Then we must add the labour of Africans and Asians. And finally, we must take into account the European workers, in Europe and elsewhere, whose labour was part of or tied to the extra-European economy. By this, admittedly speculative, reasoning, free and unfree workers in the colonial economy of the late 16th century were providing as much or more surplus value and accumulated capital for European protocapitalism than were the workers of Europe itself.

Little is known about the American workforce in the 16th century, but, again, some speculations are possible. Las Casas asserted that three million or more Indians had been enslaved by the Spaniards in Middle America during the first half of the 16th century, and this figure, once dismissed, is now taken seriously (Semo, 1975). It is known that more than 400,000 people were enslaved in Nicaragua alone (Radell, 1976). It is realized also that Indian slave labour was very important in the European economy of the Americas in that period, in Brazilian sugar planting, Mesoamerican and Antillean mining, and elsewhere. Let us speculate that 100,000 Indians were working as slaves for Europeans in a given year in the mid-16th century. Possibly 20,000 Indians were working in the mines of

Mexico and the Andes as free and forced labour in the latter part of the century (Bakewell, 1984) and it is safe to assume that five times that number were involved in the mining economy overall. Potosí, the great Andean silver-mining center, had a population of 120,000 in the 1570s (larger than Paris) (Galeano, 1973). A much greater but unknown number of Indians worked on haciendas and other European enterprises, or provided periodic forced labour, or provided tribute and rent in kind (Van Young, 1983). (The Cortés encomienda in Mexico included 50,000 Indians: Semo, 1975.) There may have been 100,000 African slaves in the Americas and So Tome in the closing years of the century. (See Curtin, 1969; Furtado, 1963; Deerr, 1949-50; Florescano, 1984; Inikori, 1979; and McAlister, 1984 for various calculations.) There may have been 300,000 Europeans, Mulattos, and Mestizos in the Americas in 1570 (McAlister, 1984), of whom conceivably 200,000 were workers. Perhaps it would not be unreasonable to estimate that one million people were working in the European economy of the Western Hemisphere in the closing years of the century, perhaps half of them engaged in productive labour in distinctly capitalist enterprises. Can this have been more than the European protocapitalist workforce of the time? (The question whether slave labour is or is not proletarian, a serious issue in discussions of the slave plantation system — see Mintz, 1985 — does not affect the basic argument of this paper.) All of this is speculation, but it points toward the conclusion that American labour was a massive part of the total labour involved in protocapitalist enterprise in the 16th century. And to all of this we must add three additional quantities: labour involved in the slave trade within continental Africa (about which very little is yet known, and about which there is much controversy at the levels of fact and concept); labour in other non-European regions (São Tomé, Ternate, Calicut, etc.) which was incorporated into the European economy or produced goods for trade to Europeans; and the labour of European workers, both inside and outside of Europe, which was part of the extra-European economy: sailors, soldiers, stevedores, teamsters, clerks, foremen, and the rest.

By the end of the 16th century the rise of Europe had well begun. As capital flowed into Europe, and as other effects of colonial enterprise also flowed into the European system or region, secondary causation appeared, including agricultural expansion and transformation, primitive manufacturing, urbanization, and expansion of rural settlements and the commercial economy. These latter have been looked at carefully but in a mainly tunnel-historical framework; as a result, the rise of Europe in the 16th century has appeared to be a process taking place wholly within the European spatial system, and caused wholly (or mainly) by autochthonous forces. As we have seen, this is an inaccurate picture and an incomplete one. Urbanization was taking place but mainly in areas connected to the extra-European economy. Inflation was also (with some qualifications) most severe in these areas (Fisher, 1989). Among the sectors of the European economy which were growing in the 16th century, some, like piracy (Dunn, 1972: 10-11) and shipbuilding, were tied directly to the extra-European economy, while others, like wheat production and North-Atlantic fishing, were stimulated directly and indirectly by that economy.

I would generalize as follows. The initiating condition, at the beginning of the 16th century, is a West- and Central-European economy which is undergoing slow but definite change toward capitalism — as are many regions of Asia and Africa at this time. Novel forces intrude into the European system, as impinging boundary processes, because of the conquest and the other extra-European events, intruding processes which consist mainly of capital and material products (and of course the dead labour embedded in these things). These than intersect with the ongoing evolving economic, technological, demographic, etc., changes. Many new changes appear, as a result not of direct stimulus from the extra-European world but of the changes already underway which, themselves, are results of those boundary processes. The internal European changes of course feed forward to produce intensification of the processes going on in America, Africa, and Asia, and these, in turn, produce still more changes within Europe. There was a tendency for major economic changes to occur first near the mercantile-maritime centers which participated in the extra-European processes. Obviously, not all of the centers which existed in 1492 were equal participants in that process, with some of the Iberian, Italian, and Flemish port cities taking the lead. But the network was sufficiently tight so that Baltic and English ports were early participants, as were inland cities with special economic characteristics, like Augsburg and Paris. From these many centers, the process spread into the interior of Europe, first into areas which supplied basic staple goods like wheat — the explosive growth at that time of the Baltic wheat trade and the manorial production of wheat in parts of Central and East Europe is well-known — and then elsewhere.

Other processes were underway as well, of course, so the pattern mapped out here is much too simple. Population growth in some areas reflected 16th-century economic changes but in other areas it signified recovery from 14th-and 15th-century population declines. Other changes, such as peasant revolts, reflected the general crisis of the late feudal economy, but the 16th-century rise of prices and (in some areas) rents was a contributing force in the unrest. As to the Reformation, and setting aside the questions concerning prior religious struggles which culminated in the 16th-century Reformation, I would argue in the Tawneyan tradition that it was broadly an effect, not an independent cause, of the economic changes that were taking place in Europe in the 16th century. But which changes? The internal crumbling of feudalism? The forces suddenly impinging from the extra-European world? Both? Probably the spatial diffusion of the Reformation in the 16th century reflected mainly intra-

European forces (Hannemann, 1975), but there is no question that, by the time of the 17th-century bourgeois revolutions, many of the areas most deeply involved in extra-European accumulation activities tended to be centers also of Protestantism. In sum: the spatial patterns of change in 16th-century Europe reflect to some extent the integration of Europe with America, and secondarily Africa and Asia, but the pattern is still somewhat obscure.

Overall, the processes of transformation and modernization in 16th-century Europe were terribly complex, varying in time and place throughout most of that continent. But the generalization is nonetheless fairly straightforward. The extra-European component, after 1492, led to an immense stimulation of changes in Europe, those which produced on the one hand an increase in the rate of European economic change and growth, on the other hand a centration of capitalism in Europe — instead of Egypt or China or some other region, or many regions at the same time.

The Seventeenth Century. By the middle of the 17th century, changes were taking place in Europe at a rapid rate and on a massive scale, and the problem of sorting out the internal and external causes and effects for this period is a very complex matter. In this same period there occurred a massive expansion, in location and intensity, of formal and informal colonialism in the Americas and around the coasts of Africa and Asia, and for these extra-European processes the problem of complexity is compounded by a lack of quantitative data as to volume of production, numbers in the labour forces, capital accumulation, and other information that would help us to judge the role of colonialism (as a broad concept) in the changes which were taking place within Europe. These matters are far too complex to permit us to discuss them satisfactorily in this short essay. I will limit myself to a brief comment.

By the beginning of the 17th century, the Netherlands and England had begun to emerge as the centers (or center) of capitalist development in Europe. Although Spain continued to feed huge quantities of silver and some gold into Europe in the first half of this century, and Portuguese plantations in Brazil and trading activities in Asia continued to be important fountains of accumulation, the main expansion of colonial enterprise after 1600 was Dutch and English. The crucial component was the West Indian plantation system, which expanded explosively after about 1640. (Fifty thousand slaves were imported into Barbados alone in the following 50 years. Probably two *million* slaves were imported into the Americas in the course of the 17th century. See Deerr, 1949-50; Curtin, 1969; Inikori, 1979.) If we place the Dutch and British sugar colonies in the same economic space as the metropolitan countries themselves, it seems likely that the sugar plantation economy was the single largest productive sector in this expanded European economy aside from family farming, and by far the largest single generator of surplus value. (Brazilian plantations, producing partly for Dutch capital, were still, in the mid-17th century, more massive than the West Indian.) But British and Dutch enterprise in the Eastern Hemisphere was also expanding very rapidly; the East India companies were formed around 1600, and by 1650 the Dutch and British together controlled most of the intercontinental trade — unequal trade, and in a sense semi-colonial — with Asia as well as the slave trade in Africa. Meanwhile, Spanish enterprise was yielding substantial accumulation in America (whether or not there was a '17th-century depression'). To all of this must be added a great variety of additional extra-European sources of accumulation: a now massive fishing industry in the northwestern Atlantic, resource extraction and the beginnings of European settlement in North America, the slave trade, piracy, Russian enterprise in Siberia, and much more.

The key question is: How central was the role played by colonial and semi-colonial enterprise in the 17th-century rise of Europe and of capitalism within Europe? There was, to begin with, a continuation and enlargement of the 16th-century processes. By the middle of the next century the European bourgeoisie had strengthened their class position, had enticed much of the feudal aristocracy into joining bourgeois enterprise, and had well begun the process of destroying proto-capitalist enterprise outside of Europe, as a result basically of the inflowing capital from America (and secondarily in that period, Africa and Asia). Now, apart from stocks of precious metal, it is improbable that capital accumulated from extra-European enterprise in 1500-1650 amounted to a sizeable share of total invested capital in Europe, even in the more advanced regions of Europe, even in the economic sectors in which capital was more or less fluid. What it did was provide a critical increment: everywhere it allowed the protocapitalist community to offer higher prices for products, labour, and land; everywhere it put investment capital in the hands of classes and communities other than the traditional elite, the group less likely to accumulate beyond its social needs and less likely to reinvest profits in new ventures. Colonial capital, in a word, was new capital. Without it, the sluggish late-medieval economy of pre-1492 days would have continued its slow progress out of feudalism and toward capitalism (or something similar), but there would have been no Seventeenth Century Bourgeois Revolution.

Growth now did not involve technological change in any important way: production increases were mainly matters of drawing more workers and more productive materials into traditional productive processes to yield more output. The capitalists had access to labour — at the levels of production then prevailing a truly massive proletarianization was not necessary — and had access to raw materials (some European, some colonial). The growth of capitalist enterprise in that period was perhaps constrained most seriously by the need to open up new markets: to sell more of the product so that more could be produced, more capital accumulated, and so on. Some of these markets were in Europe itself. But probably the main growth of markets for proto-capitalist enterprise in the 17th century, and thus the main stimulus now for the rise of capitalism, was outside of the system. This is well-known in the case of trade with Eastern Europe. It is known in the case of markets in America, Africa, and Asia, but the quantitative significance of these extra-European markets has not been fully evaluated.

In the 17th century, then, the most crucial role of the extra-European world was, I think, to permit an expansion of demand — including forced demand, as on the slave plantations — for capitalist products sufficiently great so that productive capacity and output of capitalist enterprises could grow at an increasingly fast rate. This growth in output was one of the two essential 17th-century forces involved in the rise of capitalism. The second force was, simply, the political triumph itself, the bourgeois revolution or revolutions. This provided the bourgeoisie with the legal and political power to rip apart the fabric of the society in its quest for accumulation. Forced proletarianization thereby became possible, as did government support for almost any strategy which the capitalists had in mind. And an industrial revolution, a transformation of the methods of production so that output could increase at an even greater rate, became (one might say) inevitable.

Conclusion

The argument of this essay is simple: There was no 'European miracle'. Africa, Asia, and Europe shared equally in the rise of capitalism prior to 1492. After 1492 Europe took the lead because of that continent's location near America and because of the immense wealth obtained through colonialism in America and elsewhere, not because Europeans were brighter or bolder or better than non-Europeans, or more modern, or more progressive, or more rational. These are myths of Eurocentric diffusionism and are best forgotten.

Acknowledgements
I wish to thank Abdul Alkalimat, América Sorrentini de
Blaut, Peter Taylor, Ben Wisner, and Wilbur Zelinsky for
their profoundly helpful suggestions and criticisms.

References

Abel, W. (1980). *Agricultural Fluctuations in Europe from
the 13th to the 20th Centuries*. London: Methuen.

Abu–Lughod, J. (1987–88). The shape of the world system
in the 13th century. *Studies in Comparative
International Development* 22, 4, 3–25.

Abu–Lughod, J. (1989). *Before European Hegemony: The
World System A.D. 1250–1350*. New York: Oxford
University Press.

Alavi, H. (1982). India: the transition to colonial capitalism. In *Capitalism and Colonial Production* (H. Alavi,
ed). London: Croom Helm.

Amin, S. (1976). *Unequal Development*. New York:
Monthly Review.

Amin, S. (1985). Modes of production: history and unequal
development. *Science and Society* 49, 2, 194-207.

Anderson, P. (1974a). *Passages from Antiquity to
Feudalism*. London: NLB.

Anderson, P. (1974b). *Lineages of the Absolute State*.
London: NLB.

Appadorai, A. (1936). *Economic Conditions in Southern
India (1000–1500 A.D.)*. Madras: University of Madras
Press.

Aston, T., and Philpin, C., eds. (1985). *The Brenner Debate*.
Cambridge: Cambridge University Press.

Atwell, W. (1982). International bullion flows and the
Chinese economy circa 1530–1650. *Past and Present*
no. 95, 68–91.

Baechler, J., Hall, J., and Mann, M., eds. (1988). *Europe
and the Rise of Capitalism*. Oxford: Blackwell.

Bakewell, P. (1984). Mining in colonial America. In *The*

Cambridge History of Latin America: Colonial Latin America (L. Bethell, ed). Cambridge: Cambridge University Press.

Blaut, J. (1976). Where was capitalism born? *Antipode* 8, 2, 1-11.

Blaut, J. (1977). Two views of diffusion. *Annals of the Association of American Geographers* 67, 343-349.

Blaut, J. (1987a). Diffusionism: A uniformitarian critique. *Annals of the Association of American Geographers* 77, 30–47.

Blaut, J. (1987b). *The National Question: Decolonizing the Theory of Nationalism.* London: Zed Books.

Blaut, J. (1989a). Colonialism and the rise of capitalism. *Science and Society* 53, 260–296.

Blaut, J. (1989b). Review of Baechler, J., et al., eds., *Europe and the Rise of Capitalism. Progress in Human Geography* 13, 441–448.

Blaut, J. (Forthcoming). Diffusionism, tunnel history, and the myth of the European miracle. In *Person, Place, Thing* (M. Eliot Hurst & S. Wong,eds).

Borah, W., and Cook, S. (1972). La demografía histórica de América Latina: necesidades y perspectivas. In *La historia económica en América Latina* (J. Bazant et al. ed). Mexico D.F.: Sep–Setentas.

Brading, D., and Cross, H. (1972). Colonial silver mining: Mexico and Peru. *Hispanic–American Historical Review* 52, 545–79.

Braudel, F. (1967). Prices in Europe from 1450 to 1750. In The *Cambridge Economic History of Europe: vol. 4.: The Economy of Expanding Europe in the 16th and 17th centuries* (E. Rich and C. Wilson, eds) pp. 378-486. Cambridge: Cambridge University Press.

Bray, F. (1984). *Agriculture.* Vol 6:2 of Needham, et al., *Science and Civilization in China.* Cambridge: Cambridge University Press.

Brenner, R. (1976). Agrarian class structure and economic development in preindustrial Europe. *Past and Present* no. 70, 30-75.

Brenner, R. (1977). The origins of capitalist development:

A critique of Neo–Smithian Marxism. *New Left Review* 104, 25–93.

Brenner, R. (1982). Agrarian roots of European capitalism. *Past and Present* no. 97.

Brenner, R. (1986). The social basis of economic development. In *Analytical Marxism* (J. Roemer, ed). Cambridge: Cambridge University Press.

Céspedes, G. (1974). *Latin America: The Early Years*. New York: Knopf.

Chandra, B. (1981). Karl Marx: His theories of Asian societies, and colonial rule. *Review* 5, 13–94.

Chaudhary, A. (1974). *Early Medieval Village in North–eastern India (A.D. 600–1200)*. Calcutta: Punthi Pustak.

Chaudhuri, S. (1974). Textile trade and industry in Bengal Suba, 1650–1720. *Indian Historical Review* 1, 262–278.

Chaudhuri, K. N. (1985). *Trade and Civilization in the Indian Ocean*. Cambridge: Cambridge University Press.

Chaunu, H., and Chaunu, P. (1956). *Séville et l'Atlantique*. Paris: SEVPEN.

Chicherov, A. (1976). On the multiplicity of socio–economic structures in India in the 17th and 18th century. *In New Indian Studies by Soviet scholars* (G. Abramov, ed). Moscow: USSR Academy of Sciences.

Corbridge, S. (1986). *Capitalist World Development*. Totowa, N.J.: Rowman and Littlefield.

Crosby, A. W. (1972). *The Columbian Exchange: Biological and Cultural Consequences of 1492*. Westport: Greenwood Publishers.

Cross, H. (1983). South American bullion production and export 1550–1750. In *Precious Metals and the Later Medieval and Early Modern Worlds* (J. Richards, ed) pp. 397–424. Durham NC: Carolina Academic Press.

Das Gupta, A. (1967). *Malabar in Asian Trade: 1740–1800*. Cambridge: Cambridge University Press.

de Vries, J. (1984). *European Urbanization, 1500–1800*. Cambridge MA: Harvard University Press.

Deerr, N. (1949–50). *The History of Sugar*. London:

Chapman and Hall, 2 vols.

Denevan, W., ed. (1976). *The Native Population of the Americas in 1492*. Madison: University of Wisconsin Press.

Devisse, J., and Labib, S. (1984). Africa in intercontinental relations. In *UNESCO General History of Africa, Vol. 4: Africa in the 12th to the 16th centuries* (D. Niane ed) pp. 635–672. London: Heinemann.

Dobb, M. (1947). *Studies in the Development of Capitalism*. New York: International Publishers.

Dunn, R. S. (1972). *Sugar and Slaves: the Rise of the Planter Class in the West Indies, 1624–1713*. Chapel Hill: University of North Carolina Press.

Edel, M. (1969). The Brazilian sugar cycle of the 17th century and the rise of West Indian competition. *Caribbean Studies* 9, 1, 24–45.

Elvin, M. (1973). *The Pattern of the Chinese Past*. Stanford: Stanford University Press.

Elvin, M. (1988). China as a counterfactual. In *Europe and the Rise of Capitalism* (J. Baechler et al., eds). Oxford: Blackwell.

Engels, F. (1970). *The Origin of the Family, Private Property, and the State*. Moscow: Progress Publisher.

Engels, F. (1975). Letter to K. Marx, June 6, 1853. *Marx and Engels Selected Correspondence* (Moscow: Progress Publisher.

Fei, Hsiao-tung (1953). *China's Gentry*. Chicago: University of Chicago Press.

Filesi, T. ed. (1972). *China and Africa in the Middle Ages*. London: Frank Cass.

Fisher, D. (1989). The price revolution: a monetary interpretation. *Journal of Economic History* 49, 883–902.

Florescano, E. (1984). The formation and economic structure of the hacienda in New Spain. In *Cambridge History of Latin America, vol. 2: Colonial Latin America* (L. Bethell, ed). Cambridge: Cambridge University Press.

Frank, A. G. (1968). *Capitalism and Underdevelopment in Latin America*. New York: Monthly Review Press.

Freund, J. (1969). *The Sociology of Max Weber*. New York: Vintage.

Furtado, C. (1963). *The Economic Growth of Brazil*. Berkeley and Los Angeles: University of California Press.

Galeano, E. (1972). *The Open Veins of Latin America*. New York: Monthly Review Press.

Galloway, J. H. (1989). *The Sugar Cane Industry: an Historical Geography from its Origins to 1914*. Cambridge: Cambridge University Press.

Gopal, L. (1963). Quasi–manorial rights in ancient India. *Journal of the Economic and Social History of the Orient* 6, 296-308.

Habib, I. (1963). *The Agrarian System of Mughal India* . London: Asia Publishing House.

Hall, J. (1985). *Powers and Liberties: the Causes and Consequences of the Rise of the West*. Oxford: Blackwell.

Hall, J. (1988). States and societies: The miracle in historical perspective. In *Europe and the Rise of Capitalism* (J. Baechler, et al. eds). Oxford: Blackwell.

Hamilton, E. J. (1929). American treasure and the rise of capitalism. *Economica* 9, 338–357.

Hamilton, E. J. (1934). *American Treasure and the Price Revolution in Spain, 1501–1650*. Cambridge: Harvard University Press.

Hamilton, G. S. (1985). Why no capitalism in China? Negative questions in historical, comparative research. *Journal of Developing Societies* 1, 187–211.

Hannemann, M. (1975). *The Diffusion of the Reformation in Southwestern Germany*. Chicago: University of Chicago Geography Department.

Harrison, P. (1969). *The Communists and Chinese Peasant Rebellions*. New York: Atheneum.

Hasan, A. (1969). The silver currency output of the Mughal Empire and prices in India during the 16th and 17th centuries. *Indian Economic and Social History Review* 6, 85–116.

Hilton, R., ed. (1976). *The Transition from Feudalism to Capitalism*. London: NLB.

Hodgett, A. J. (1972). *A Social and Economic History of Medieval Europe*. London: Methuen.

Hoyle, R. W. (1990). Tenure and the land market in early modern England: or a late contribution to the Brenner debate. *Economic History Review* 43, 1–20.

Inikori, J., ed. (1979). *The African Slave Trade from the 15th to the 19th Century*. Paris: UNESCO.

Isichei, E. (1983). *A History of Nigeria*. London: Longmans.

Jones, E. L. (1981). *The European Miracle*. Cambridge: Cambridge University Press.

Kea, R. (1982). *Settlements, Trade, and Polities in the Seventeenth–Century Gold Coast*. Baltimore: Johns Hopkins Press.

Kosambi, D. D. (1969). *Ancient India*. New York: Meridian Books.

Lewis, A. (1973). Maritime skills in the Indian Ocean, 1368–1500. *Journal of the Economic and Social History of the Orient* 16, 238–64.

Liceria, M. A. C. (1974). Emergence of Brahmanas as landed intermediaries in Karnataka, c.A.D. 1000–1300. *Indian Historical Review* 1, 28–35.

Lopez, R. (1953). Hard times and investment in culture. In *The Renaissance: A symposium* (R. Lopez, ed). New York: Metropolitan Museum of Art.

Lopez, R., and Miskimin, H. (1961–62). The economic depression of the Renaissance. *Economic History Review* 14, 408–26.

Löwith, K. (1982). *Max Weber and Karl Marx*. London: Allen and Unwin.

Ma–Huan. (1970). *The Overall Survey of the Ocean's Shores*. Cambridge: Cambridge University Press.

Magalhães–Godinho, V. (1969). *L'economie de l'empire portugais aux XV et XVI siècles*. Paris: SEVPEN.

Mahalingam, T. (1951). *Economic Life of the Vijayanegara Empire*. Madras: University of Madras Press.

Mann, M. (1986). *The Sources of Social Power, vol. 1: The History of Power from the Beginning to A.D. 1760*. Cambridge: Cambridge University Press.

Mann, M. (1988). European development: approaching a

historical explanation. In *Europe and the Rise of Capitalism* (J. Baechler, et al., eds). Oxford: Blackwell.

Marx, K. (1976). *Capital.* New York: Vintage.

Marx, K., and Engels, F. (1976). *The German Ideology.* Moscow: Progress Publishers.

Marx, K. (1979). The British rule in India. *Marx and Engels: Collected Works* (New York: International Publishers.

Matveiev, V. (1984). The development of Swahili civilization. In *UNESCO General History of Africa, Vol. 4: Africa in the 12th to the 16th centuries* (D. Niane, ed). London: Heinemann.

Minchinton, W. (1969). *The Growth of English Overseas Trade.* London: Methuen.

Mintz, S. W. (1985). *Sweetness and Power: the Place of Sugar in Modern History.* New York: Penguin.

Miskimin, H. (1969). *The Economy of Early Renaissance Europe, 1300–1460.* Englewood Cliffs: Prentice–Hall.

McAlister, L. (1984). *Spain and Portugal in the New World, 1492–1700.* Minneapolis: University of Minnesota Press.

Naqvi, H. K. (1968). *Urban Centres in Upper India, 1556–1803.* Bombay: Asia Publishing House.

Needham, J. and collaborators. (1954–). *Science and Civilization in China.* Eight vols. to date. Cambridge: Cambridge University Press.

Newsom, L. (1985). Indian population patterns in colonial Latin America. *Latin American Research Review* 20, 3, 41–74.

Niane, D. (1984). Conclusion. In *UNESCO General History of Africa, Vol. 4: Africa in the 12th to the 16th centuries* (D. Niane, ed). London: Heinemann.

Nicholas, D. M. (1967–68). Town and countryside: Social and economic tensions in 14th–century Flanders. *Comparative Studies in Society and History* 10, 458–85.

Panikkar, K. M. (1959). *Asia and Western Influence.* London: Allen and Unwin.

Parsons, J. B. (1970). *Peasant Rebellions of the Late Ming*

Dynasty. Tucson: University of Arizona Press.

Purcell, V. (1965). *The Chinese in Southeast Asia* (2nd ed.). London: Oxford University Press.

Qaisar, A. J. (1974). The role of brokers in Medieval India. *Indian Historical Review* 1, 220–46.

Radell, D. R. (1976). The Indian slave trade of Nicaragua during the 16th century. In *The Native Population of the Americas in 1492* (W. Denevan, ed).

Rawski, E. (1972). *Agricultural Change and the Peasant Economy of South China*. Cambridge: MIT Press.

Raychaudhuri, T. (1962). *Jan Company in Coromandel*. The Hague: Nijhoff.

Semo, E. (1982). *Historia del capitalismo en México: Los orígines, 1521–1763*. Mexico: Ediciones Era.

Sharma, R. S. (1965). *Indian Feudalism, c.300–1200*. Calcutta: University of Calcutta Press.

Simkin, C. (1968). *The Traditional Trade of Asia*. London: Oxford University Press.

Simonsen, R. (1944). *História economica do Brasil, 1500–1820* (2nd ed.). São Paulo: Companhia editora nacional.

Smith, C. T. (1969). *An Historical Geography of Western Europe Before 1800*. London: Longmans.

Smith, A. (1971). The early states of the Central Sudan. In *History of West Africa, Vol. 1*. (J. Ajayi and M. Crowder, eds), pp. 158–201. New York: Columbia University Press.

So, Kwan–wai. (1975). *Japanese Piracy in Ming China During the 16th century*. East Lansing: Michigan State University Press.

Sweezy, P. (1976). A critique. In *The Transition from Feudalism to Capitalism* (R. Hilton ed.).

Thorndyke, L. (1943). Renaissance or prenaissance? *Journal of the History of Ideas* 4, 65–74.

Torras, J. (1980). Class struggle in Catalonia. *Review*, 4, 253–65.

Tung, C. (1979). *An Outline History of China*. Hong Kong: Joint Publishing Co.

Udovitch, A. L. (1962). At the origins of Western

Commenda: Islam, Israel, Byzantium. *Speculum* 37, 198–207.

Van Young, E. (1983). Mexican rural history since Chevalier: The historiography of the colonial hacienda. *Latin American Research Review* 28, 3, 5–61.

Vilar, P. (1976). *A History of Gold and Money, 1450–1920*. London: NLB.

Vives, J. V. (1969). *An Economic History of Spain*. Princeton: Princeton University Press.

Wachtel, N. (1984). The Indian and Spanish Conquest. *Cambridge History of Latin America: Colonial Latin America, Vol. 1.* (L. Bethell, ed). Cambridge: Cambridge University Press.

Wallerstein, I. (1974). *The Modern World System*. New York: Academic Press.

Watson, A. (1983). *Agricultural Innovation in the Early Islamic World: the Diffusion of Crops and Farming Techniques, 700–1100*. Cambridge: Cambridge University Press.

Webb, W. P. (1951). *The Great Frontier*. Austin: University of Texas Press.

Weber, M. (1951). *The Religion of China*. New York: Free Press.

Weber, M. (1958). *The Protestant Ethic and the Spirit of Capitalism*. New York: Scribner's.

Weber, M. (1967). *The Religion of India*. New York: Free Press.

Weber, M. (1981). *General Economic History*. New Brunswick: Transaction Books.

White, L., jr. (1962). *Medieval Technology and Social Change*. London: Oxford University Press.

White, L., jr. (1968). *Machina Ex Deo: Essays in the Dynamism of Western Culture*. Cambridge, MA: MIT Press.

Wiethoff, B. (1963). *Die Chinesische Seeverbotspolitik und der Private Überseehandel von 1368 bis 1567*. Hamburg: Gesellschaft für Natur– und Völkerkunde Ostasiens.

Wittfogel, K. (1957). *Oriental Despotism*. New Haven: Yale

University Press.
Yadava, B. (1974). Immobility and subjugation of Indian peasantry in early medieval complex. *Indian Historical Review* 1, 18–74.

Fourteen Ninety-two Once Again

Andre Gunder Frank

University of Amsterdam

It is an embarrassing pleasure for me to comment. A pleasure; because I agree, and then some. Embarrassing; because I have written much the same, and then some, but with qualifications. For present purposes, J. M. Blaut's rich essay may be summarized as a main thesis, which in turn rests on two sub-theses, on which I shall comment here. The main thesis is that (Western) European (capitalist) development was not due to characteristics that were specifically inherent in, or processes that were limited to, Europe. That is incontrovertible from a world historical perspective, however much this obvious fact may be neglected or denied by the authors from Marx and Weber to Brenner and Jones, whom Blaut rightly rebuts. Whatever the ideological motives, some of which Blaut considers, of their Eurocentric tunnel vision, it requires rejection for its nefarious consequences.

The two sub-theses supporting the main one are (in reverse order of his presentation):
1. After 1492 and particularly until 1700, the development of [Western] Europe was materially based on capital accumulation through its exploitation of the Western

Hemisphere in the 'New World'.
2. Before 1492, European development was not significantly different from, but part of an 'Old World' Eastern-
hemispheric-wide development.

For Blaut, these two sub-theses also generate that additional derivative [sub?] thesis:

3. '1492 represents the breakpoint between two fundamentally different evolutionary epochs'.

I also accept the two sub-theses, but I no longer think
that they necessarily signify the validity of the third one.

After 1492

The argument that after 1492 European development
[of capitalism] benefited from capital accumulation based
on its exploitation of the Americas has been made before,
among others by Smith, Marx and Keynes. Twenty years
ago I also made this argument from a world (capitalist)
system perspective, later published under the title *World
Accumulation 1492-1789*:

> In summary then, we may say that the sixteenth
> century witnessed the first long, sustained, and
> widespread quantitative and qualitative develop-
> ment of capitalism in its mercantile stage and the
> first period of concentrated capital accumulation in
> Europe . . . The same process extended far beyond
> Europe to those regions or 'enclaves' which were
> integrated into the process of world capital accumu-
> lation at this stage, especially the New World
> sources of gold and silver. During this sixteenth-
> century secular and cyclical upswing, western
> Europe experienced a .sharp acceleration of the
> process of capital accumulation... The indigenous

population of the New World suffered yet more from the contribution to the process of primitive capital accumulation during the sixteenth century . . The precious metals from the New World enabled Western European countries to settle directly or indirectly the deficit in the trade balance with the Orient (Frank, 1978a 52 53, 63).

Therefore, I welcome Blaut's elaboration of this thesis since 1976 and again in the present essay. I also welcome his attempt to quantify some of the (oft underestimated) surplus contributed to accumulation in Europe by (forced) labor in the New World, and his argument that the capture of this surplus enhanced [West] European ability to compete with East Europeans and Asians—and then to out-compete them—in the world economy. The book cited above, and its companion volume, *Dependent Accumulation and Underdevelopment* (Frank, 1987b), were my attempts to analyze this same world capitalist development and its uneven cyclical process in its unequal center-periphery structure of the world .system. However, then I still thought that it all started in 1492, and that is why I put that date in my title.

Before 1492

Blaut's other sub-thesis is that 'it' did not start in 1492, but much earlier, though he does not say when. I now agree with him. However, I now go much farther still than he— in time, back to at least 3000 B.C.; in scope, to all of Afro-Eurasia for most of this time; and in depth, about the 5000-year 'cumulation of accumulation' in a single world system.

I welcome rejections and disqualifications of Eurocentrism. As long ago as 1978, 1 agreed with Blaut that in 1492 Europe still enjoyed no particular advantages:

> In the sixteenth century then, the level of techno-
> logical and economic development of the trading
> partners was still qualitatively equivalent, and
> trade between Europeans and Africans was carried
> out to the mutual benefit and with the mutual
> respect of both Innumerable surviving letters and
> other documents bear witness to the admiration of
> many European visitors for the cultural advance-
> ment of the African peoples. . . . A further testimo-
> nial from the Elizabethan era is Shakespeare's
> treatment of Othello (Frank, 1978a: 39).

Neither then nor now did or does it seem to me to be
worth the trouble to 'argue' against theses that knowing-
ly or unknowingly attribute 'superior' environmental,
racial, cultural or other characteristics to Europeans, or
which attribute Europe's (temporary) position in the world
to such supposed innate characteristics. Despite Blaut's
citation of Eurocentric chapter and verse from many
authors, including personal friends of mine, detailed
analysis and rebuttal of this sort of essentially racist litany
strikes me as unworthy. It seems to me sufficient to refer
Eurocentrists and others to demonstrations by Westerners
(whose testimony Eurocentrism presumably cannot dis-
qualify out of hand) such as Needham (1954-84) and
McNeill (1983) of the earlier superiority of China's technology and economy, or of Islamic culture and economy
by Hodgson (1974) and Lombard (1975). More recently,
Bernal (1987) and Amin (1988), the latter under the title
Eurocentrism, have already pulled out the rug from under
its *ideological* foundation. In his excellent critique of Perry
Anderson and others, Teshale Tibebu (1990: 83-85, emphasis in original) also argues (persuasively to me and probably to Blaut) that much of their analysis of 'Feudalism,
Absolutism and the Bourgeois Revolution' and 'their obses-
sion with the .specificity ... [and] supposed superiority of
Europe' is Western 'civilization arrogance', 'ideology
dressed up as history' and *'Orientalism painted red'*, that

is the *'continuation of orientalism by other means*. The other means is provided by theoretical Marxism'.

That done, our time seems better invested in trying to reconstruct a reading of the history of the world before 1492 'wie es eigentlich gewesen ist' [as it really was]. Blaut is able to devote only little attention in this article to 'links [that] had been forged over many centuries . . . even when China traded with Rome'. He summarizes that 'the mercantile-maritime, protocapitalist centers of the Eastern Hemisphere were connected tightly with one another in networks—ultimately a single network—along which flowed material things, people and ideas' (Blaut, 1976). Over the past couple of years, one of my own endeavors has been more systematically to study these links or this ultimately single network as the developement of a single world system. its structure and process are set out in Frank (1990a, 1990b, 1991a, 1991b, 1992a and 1992b); in Gills and Frank (1990, 1991a, 1991b); and in Frank and Gills (1992a and 1992b). The main arguments will hopefully soon appear as a book (Frank and Gills, 1992b). They are summarized under the title 'A plea for world system history', which begins

> I plead for writing a world history that is as comprehensive and systematic as possible. It should offer a more humanocentric alternative to western Eurocentrism. This history should seek maximum 'unity in diversity' of human experience and development . . . We may also discover common features and relations among them, which are derived from their common participation in a whole, which is more than the sum of its parts. For the long period before 1492, this 'whole' world history should concentrate on the unity and historical interrelations within the Asio-Afro European 'Eastern' hemispheric ecumene, stretching from the Pacific to the Atlantic—before Columbus (again) crossed the latter. The principal idea I advance is the principle,

indeed the imperative, to do a world *system* 'macro'
history. The main reason to do so is that 'the whole
is more than the sum of its parts' (Frank, 1991a: 1).

The argument that *this same* world system was born
long before 1492 is summarized and explicated elsewhere:

> We argue that the main features of the economic
> and interstate world system already analyzed by
> Wallerstein (1974) and Modelski (1987) for the
> 'modern' world system, and for earlier ones by
> Chase-Dunn (1986,1989) and others, and in this
> book by Chase-Dunn and Hall ([1991] Chapter 1)
> and Wilkinson ([1991] Chapter 4 and also 1987)
> also characterize the development of this same
> world system in medieval and ancient times, indeed
> for at least the past five millennia. These features
> are 1) the historical continuity and development of
> a single world economy and inter-polity system; 2)
> capital accumulation, technological progress, and
> ecological adaptation degradation as the principal
> motor forces in the world system; 3) the hierarchi-
> cal center-periphery political economic structure of
> the world system; 4) alternate periods of political
> economic hegemony and rivalry (and war) in the
> world system; 5) and long political economic cycles
> of growth accumulation, center/periphery positions,
> hegemony/ rivalry, etc. Our study of the unequal
> structure and uneven dynamic of this world system
> is based, like a three legged stool, on economic,
> political, and cultural analysis (Gills and Frank,
> 1991a: 67).

Therefore, I must regard Blaut's claim as questionable
that before 1492 Eastern hemisphere development was
'even' or 'at the same rate' in different parts, and not
uneven. On the other hand, I believe we can and must trace
systemic development in the hemisphere much farther

back in history. In the introduction to Gills and Frank (1991a), we identify the following key points:

I. World Systems Origins
1. **The origins** of our present world system (WS) can and should be traced back at least 5000 years to the relations between Mesopotamia and Egypt.
2. **Economic connections** among various parts of the WS began much earlier and have been much more prevalent and significant than is often realized.
3. **World system extension** grew to include most of the Asio-Afro-European ecumenical ('Eastern' hemisphere) landmass and its out-lying islands by 600 BC and incorporated much of the 'Western' 'New World' by 1500 AD, although there is increasing evidence of earlier contacts between them.

III. Infrastructural Investment, Technology and Ecology
1. **Infrastructural investment and accumulation** accompanied and supported most parts of the WS from its beginning and throughout its historical development.
2. **Technological innovation** also played a similar and related role throughout the historical development of the WS and mediated in the competitive economic and military conflicts among its parts [and was certainly not of post 1492 European invention].

IV Surplas Transfer and Accumulation Relations
1. **Surplus transfer and inter-penetrating accumulation** among parts of the WS are its essential defining characteristics. This transfer means that no part of the WS would be as it was and is without its relations with other parts and the whole [which makes all discourse on the inherent peculiarity of Europe largely beside the point].
2. **Center—Periphery—Hinterland** (CPH) complexes and hierarchies among different peoples, regions and

classes have always been an important part of WS structure. However, the occupancy of musical chair places within this structure has frequently changed and contributed to the dynamics of WS historical development [and would also give rise to the 'Rise of the West' after 1492].

Therefore, I agree with Blaut when he denies the ideology of 'the European miracle'. I also join him in 'parting company with traditional Marxists who, like traditional conservatives, believe the rise of capitalism is to be explained by processes internal to Europe. Strictly speaking, there was no 'transition from feudalism to capitalism in Europe'. I welcome Blaut's pursuit of Eurasian-wide developments and their repercussions in Europe before 1492. However, I think we must go much further, and we should part company with still more beliefs, including some of Blaut's own about capitalism, as we will see below. This position has been developed elsewhere (Frank, 1991b) as seven real world system issues and proposals. For understanding this and subsequent transitions, therefore, we should:

1. **Abandon the schema of a 'European' world (system)** and look outside. Wallerstein and so many others look out the window from their European house; but they still cannot see its (still marginal) place in the world landscape. Why are the Mongols 'the link' in a Chinese-Islamic 'trading world-system' before 1500, yet Wallerstein and others still refuse to accept the prior existence of this **system?**
2. **Look at the whole world system.** China, the Mongols, the Islamic world, and Europe, not to mention other parts of the Asio-Afro-European ecumene were linked into a trading and inter-state working .system in the thirteenth century, à la Abu-Lughod. Should we recognize that this was **the world system** out of whose crisis hegemonial European capitalism emerged? Posing

the right question is getting more than half of the right answer.

3. **Recognize long cycles of development in this world system.** Wallerstein recognizes that 'it is the long swing that is crucial': '1050-1250 up-swing and 1250-1450 downswing . . . and 1450-1600 long sixteenth century' (renewed) upswing, before the renewed '.seventeenth century crisis'. Moreover, Wallerstein [1989] recognizes that it was the 'crisis' during the 1250-1450 downturn that led to 'cumulative collapse' and then to regeneration and a new 'genesis'. However, Wallerstein and others neglect to ask—and therefore to find any answer—to the crucial question: crisis, collapse, new genesis in **what system?** Of course, as George Modelski (who is also incapable of seeing **this** system, *vide* Modelski, 1987) correctly pointed out to my seminar in person, 'in order for us to look for a cycle, we must first be clear about the **system** in which this cycle occurs'. So there are two possibilities: The same European system predates 1500, or Europe was part of an (also same) world system that also predates 1500. Either way Wallerstein's and others' temporal and Eurocentric myopia blinds them to seeing the whole picture of systemic historical reality.

4. **Realize that hegemony in the world system did not begin in Europe** after 1500, but that it shifted to Europe in the course of hegemonial crises and decline in the East of the same world system. Even Wallerstein quotes Abu-Lughod (1989) that 'Before European Hegemony, the Fall of the East preceded the Rise of the West'. Abu-Lughod is at pains to show how and why the various parts of the East declined at this time in world systemic terms. Therefore, the root causes of **the rise of the West to hegemony and the transition to capitalism in Europe cannot be found within Europe alone,** but must be sought in the course of the development of the world system—and also within its

other parts—as a whole. 'If we are to understand the problematique . . . we must begin with the world system that creates it!' (quoted from Frank, 1965).

These long economic cycles and their associated hegemonial shifts within the single world system, not only since 1000 AD but back to 2000 BC and earlier, are identified and analyzed under the title 'World system cycles, crises, and hegemonial transitions' by Gills and Frank (1991b).

Is 1492 really a 'breakpoint'?

Beginning with the world system that creates the problematique of hegemonial shift and transition, however, also puts into question Blaut's derivative thesis that '1492 represents the breakpoint between two fundamentally different evolutionary epochs'. For if 1492 is a year between a world-system-wide process and structure before and after that date, then what makes it a 'breakpoint'? The answer is that for Blaut and others 1492 marks the beginning of the 'different evolutionary epoch' of *capitalism* and its North-South, center-periphery polarity in the world. However, that Eurocentric faith may be challenged too! True, the peoples of the New World were subjected for the first time to the ravages, which Blaut and his sources describe and which tragically were due primarily to their previous immunity. However, peoples had been subject to brutalities of center-periphery colonization within the world system east of the Atlantic before [and in other system(s) also in lands West of the Atlantic, to which incidentally they had apparently also migrated eastward across the Pacific and not only over the Bering Straits, as Blaut seems to think].

Blaut himself argues that Asia was not pressed into the new center periphery structure before 1700, or indeed until after industrialization in the 1800s. If so, then what else defines the 'breakpoint' in 1492? Answer: The *capitalist* mode of production. However again, Blaut also recognizes all manner of proto-capitalist features in many parts of Eurasia long before 1492. This observation raises two additional questions: What, if anything, makes the *difference* between 'real' capitalism and 'proto'-capitalism such an important breakpoint? And, whatever the answer, is it more important than the *continuity* in the world system across 1492 or any other date? As I have argued elsewhere (Frank, 1991b):

5. **Do not pursue the idea of 'proto-capitalism'** into the blind alley it is likely to be. The first supposed resolution of the feudalism-capitalism debate a quarter century ago was to try to 'compromise' on 'semi-feudalism' going on to become 'semi-' 'proto-' capitalism. I thought that this 'compromise' was a non-starter then; and experience has shown that the 'mode of production' debate detracted from better understanding of problematique analyzing the world system that creates it itself.

By the same token, Blaut's reference to 'feudalism' and its decline in various parts of Eurasia confuses more than it clarifies. As Tibebu (1990: 50) points out, 'feudalism was conceptualized by its enemies . . . long after feudalism itself had ceased to be dominant . . . The word "feudal" is almost nothing more than a synonym for the word bad. Perhaps the best analogy is the political use of the word "fascist"'. Again, as I have argued elsewhere (Frank, 1991b):

6. **Liberate ourselves from the optical illusion of the false identity of 'system' and 'mode of production'**. Samir Amin contends that the system could not have been the same system before 1500 because it did not have the capitalist mode of production, which only developed later. Before 1500, according to Amin and others, modes of production were tributary. My answer is that the **system was the same no**

matter what the mode of production was. The focus on the mode of production blinds us to seeing the more important systemic continuity. Wallerstein makes **the same confusion** between 'mode' and 'system'. Indeed *the single differentia specifica of Wallerstein's Modern World-Capitalist-System is its mode of production*. Wallerstein's identification and also confusion of 'system' and 'mode' is evident throughout his works and widely recognized by others.

7. **Therefore, also dare to abandon (the sacrosanct belief in) capitalism** as a distinct mode of production and separate system. What was the ideological reason for my and Wallerstein's 'scientific' construction of a sixteenth century transition (from feudalism in Europe) to a modern world capitalist economy and system? It was the belief in a subsequent transition from capitalism to socialism, if not immediately in the world as a whole, at least through 'socialism in one country' after another. Traditional Marxists and many others who debated with us, even more so, were intent on preserving faith in the prior but for them more recent transition from one (feudal) mode of production to another (capitalist) one. Their political ideological reason was that they were intent on the subsequent transition to still another and supposedly different socialist mode of production. That was (and is?) the position of Marxists, traditional and otherwise, like Brenner (1985) and Anderson (1974). That is still the position of Samir Amin (1991), who like Wallerstein, now wants to take refuge in 'proto-capitalism'—and by extension 'proto-socialism.'

Similarly and by extension to his above-cited argument, Tibebu suggests that the fundamental justification among almost all Marxists for the term 'bourgeois revolution' is an argument based on an analogy to the long-awaited proletarian revolution: 'Just as the transition from capitalism to socialism takes place through proletarian revolution, so

in the same way, it is assumed that the transition from
feudalism to capitalism must have taken place through a
bourgeois revolution' (Tibebu, 1990:122). He argues that
both revolutions are 'imaginary'—so to say, wishful thinking. So are, I submit, both 'transitions'.

> So is there still a political ideological reason to hold
> on to the fond belief In a suppose(1 'transition from
> feudalism to capitalism', around 1800, or 1500 [i.e.
> 1492], or whenever—to support the fond belief in a
> 'transition to socialism' in 1917, or 1949, or whenev-
> er? Is there any such reason still to continue look-
> ing for this earlier transition and its hegemonial
> development only in Europe, while real hegemony
> is now shifting (no doubt through the contemporary
> and near future non-hegemonic interregnum) back
> towards Asia? NO, there is none (Frank, 1991b).

Conclusion

In conclusion, in that case, we can and should well
accept Blaut's main thesis against Eurocentrism and his
two sub-theses about Europe's place in world (system) history both before and after 1492. However, we need and perhaps should *not* continue to hold on for dear life to my
earlier and his continued idea that 1492 represented a
breakpoint between *different* evolutionary epochs. For the
epochs both before and after 1492 were part of the *same*
evolutionary 'development' in the *same world system*,
which made and again unmade Europe's dominance.

References

Abu–Lughod, J. (1989). *Before European Hegemony: The World System A.D.* 1250–1350. New York: Oxford University Press.

Amin, S. (1988). *L'eurocentrisme: Critique d'une ideologie.* Paris: Anthropos. (English edn: *Eurocentrism.* New York: Monthly Review Press).

Amin, S. (1991). The ancient world–systems versus the modern world system. *Review* 14(3), 349–385.

Anderson, P. (1974). *Lineages of the Absolutist State.* London: New Left Books.

Bernal, M. (1987). *Black Athena: The Afroasiatic Roots of Classical Civilization.* New Brunswick: Rutgers University Press.

Brenner, R. (1985). In *The Brenner Debate* (T. H. Ashton and C. H. W. Philpin eds). Cambridge: Cambridge University Press.

Chase–Dunn, C. (1986). *Rise and Demise: World–systems and Modes of Production.* Boulder: Westview Press. (Forthcoming).

Chase–Dunn, C. (1989a). *Global Formation: Structures of the World–Economy.* Cambridge and Oxford: Basil Blackwell.

Chase–Dunn, C. (1989b). *Core/periphery hierarchies in the development of intersocietal networks.* (Unpublished manuscript).

Chase–Dunn, C. and Hall, T. eds (1991). *Precapitalist Core–Periphery Relations.* Boulder: Westview Press.

Frank, A. G. (1965). Con que modo de produccion convierte la gallina maiz en huevos de oro? *El Gallo Ilustrado Suplemento de El Dia, Mexico,* 31 October and 25 November. (Reprinted 1969, in *Latin America: Underdevelopment or revolution.* New York: Monthly Review Press).

Frank, A. G. (1978a). *World Accumulation 1492–1789.* New York: Monthly Review Press; London: Macmillan Press.

Frank, A. G. (1978b). *Dependent Accumulation and Underdevelopment.* New York: Monthly Review Press; London: Macmillan Press.

Frank, A. G. (1990a). A theoretical introduction to 5000 years of world system history. *Review* (Binghamton) 13(2), 155–248.

Frank, A. G. (1990b). The thirteenth century world system: a review essay. *Journal of World History* 1(2), 249–256.

Frank, A. G. (1991a). A plea for world system history. *Journal of World History* 2(1), 1–28.

Frank, A. G. (1991b). Transitional ideological modes: feudalism, capitalism, socialism. *Critique of Anthropology* 11(2). (Forthcoming).

Frank, A. G. (1992a). *The Centrality of Central Asia.* Amsterdam VU University Press for the Center for Asian Studies, Amsterdam, Comparitive Asian Studies No. 8. Also published in *Studies in History* (New Delhi), 8(1); and to be published in the *Bulletin of Concerned Asian Scholars* (Boulder, CO), 24(2).

Frank, A. G. (1992b). 1492 and Latin America at the margin of world history: East–West hegemonial shifts 992–1492–1992. Paper presented at the International Studies Association Annual Meetings, Atlanta, GA, 1–5 April 1992.

Frank, A. G. and Gills, B. K. (1992a). The five thousand year world system: an interdisciplinary introduction. *Humboldt Journal of Social Relations* (Arcata, CA) 18(2). (Forthcoming).

Frank, A. G. and Gills, B. K., eds (1992b). *The World System: From Five Hundred Years to Five Thousand.* London and New York: Routledge. (Forthcoming).

Gills, B. K. and Frank, A. G. (1990). The cumulation of accumulation: theses and research agenda for 5000 years of world system history. *Dialectical Anthropology* (New York/Amsterdam) 15, 19–42.

Gills, B. K. and Frank, A. G. (1991a). 5000 years of world system history: the cumulation of accumulation. In *Precapitalist Core–Perphery Relations* (C. Chase–Dunn and T. Hall eds) pp. 67–11. Boulder: Westview Press.

Gills, B. K. and Frank A. G. (1992). World system cycles, crises and hegemonial shifts 1700 BC to 1700 AD. *Review* 15(4). (Forthcoming).

Hodgson, M. G. S. (1974). *The Venture of Islam,* 3 vols. Chicago: University of Chicago Press.

Lombard, M. (1975). *The Golden Age of Islam.* Amsterdam: North Holland.

McNeill, W. (1983). *The Pursuit of Power: Technology, Armed Force and Society since AD 1000.* Oxford: Blackwell.

Modelski, G. (1987). *Long Cycles in World Politics.* London: Macmillan Press.

Needham, J. (1961–84). *Science and Civilization in China,* 8 vols. Cambridge: Cambridge University Press.

Thompson, W. R. (1988). *On Global War: Historical–Structural Approaches to World Politics.* Columbia, SC: University of South Carolina Press.

Tibebu, T. (1990). On the question of feudalism, absolutism, and the bourgeois revolution. *Review* 13(1).

Wallerstein, I. (1974). *The Modern World–System, Vol. I.* New York: Academic Books.

Wallerstein, I. (1989). The West, capitalism, and the modern world–system. Prepared as a chapter in J. Needham *Science and Civilization in China, Vol. VII: The Social Background,*Part 2, Sect. 48: Social and Economic Considerations. Published as L'Occident, le capitalisme, et le systeme–monde moderne. *Sociologies et Societes* (Montreal) 21(1), June 1990.

Wilkinson, D. (1987). Central civilization. *Comparative Civilizations Review* 17, Fall, 31–59.

Wilkinson, D. (1988). World–economic theories and problems: Quigley vs. Wallerstein vs. central civilization. Paper delivered at Annual Meetings of the International Society for the Comparative Study of Civilizations, 26–29 May.

Wilkinson, D. (1991). Cores, peripheries, and civilizations. In *Precapitalist Core–Periphery Relations* (C. Chase–Dunn and T. Hall eds). Boulder: Westview Press.

On Jim Blaut's 'Fourteen Ninety-two'

Samir Amin

Third World Forum, Dakar, Senegal

Blaut's 'Fourteen ninety-two' is an important contribution to the debate on the rise of capitalism. The paper follows a previous one by the same author, entitled 'Colonialism and the rise of capitalism' which I reviewed for *Science and Society* (vol. 54, no. 1,1990). As I noted previously, Blaut's two central theses converge perfectly with those which I have myself developed. These are:

1. that capitalism is not the product of an exclusive, specific conjuncture proper to the history of Europe, but it is the necessary outcome of contradictions operating in an analogous manner in all advanced pre-capitalist societies; and

2. that colonization has played from its origin—that is to say, from the conquest of America—a decisive double role, on the one hand triggering the rapid passage to capitalism in Europe and in consequence, on the other hand, brutally halting elsewhere advancements which had been going in the same direction.

In this new paper J. M. Blaut provides some additional strong arguments in favor of his theses. First, he rejects some of the main Eurocentric arguments aimed at proving the so-called exceptionality of the European line of development, which are bound to overestimate the internal class struggle between serfs and lords as well as some so-called specific 'cultural' features (Weber, Perry Anderson, Robert Brenner, etc....). I shall not come back on this critique which I wholly share, having myself developed a similar line of argument in my book, Eurocentrism (Amin, 1988). Secondly, he adds to his previous arguments in favor of the decisive role played by the colonization of America in the rise of capitalism. Indeed, Eurocentric history often plays down—and even forgets—the quantitative as well as qualitative role played by the American periphery in the mercantilist transition to industrial capitalism (the 16th, 17th and 18th centuries), such as:

1. The constant and massive flows of gold and silver from America which reinforced considerably the social position of merchants within European society and gave them an absolute advantage in their competition with the oriental traders who previously had dominated large networks of long-distance trade—the Europeans could offer better prices for all goods in all markets.

2. The importance of the plantations' profits, also often routinely underestimated. Blaut reminds us that in 1600 Brazil exported sugar with a gross value of £2,000,000, i.e. double the total value of all exports from England to all the world in that year. He indicates that the rates of profit in the plantation system were so high that production capacities could be doubled every two years.

3. The importance of American peripheral capitalism in the world system of these times. Blaut reminds us here, for instance, that Potosí had a population of 120,000 in the 1570s (larger than Paris).

4. Blaut comes back in this paper on another of his quantitative decisive calculations, that of the population directly exploited—and over-exploited—in the Americas, to the benefit of European mercantile capitalism.

In a word, Blaut shows clearly that America was not a new and additional 'trading partner' of Europe (as Oriental societies were and continued to be for some time), but was fabricated as a peripheral subaltern society playing a crucial role for capital accumulation. Enterprises in the Americas were established from the very start as a matter of profit and capital accumulation.

Finally Blaut addresses in this paper three new sets of questions:

1. The question of the 'crisis' of the mercantilist system in the 17th century. Blaut argues, convincingly, that this crisis was the result of a shift in the use of the profits extracted from the exploitation of the Americas: instead of being reinvested in western Europe itself, this surplus was channeled towards a new expansion overseas (India) and in eastern Europe.

2. To the question 'Why was America conquered by Europeans and not Africans or Asians?', Blaut argues that the answer should be sought in geography: it was easier—even by chance—to reach the Atlantic coast of America starting from the Iberian peninsula than from further south; it was much more difficult for Asians to reach America through the Pacific.

3. To the question 'Why was the conquest successful?' Blaut stresses—rightly—the fact that American native agriculture was lagging 4000 years behind that of the Old World, due to the relative isolation of the continent.

As I have said already in my previous comments on Blaut's theses, I see a parallel development of my argument with respect to the mechanisms of the law of value operating in a global context. I also repeat here that in my understanding there is no contradiction, but rather a complementarity, between the argument based on the crucial importance of colonialism in the rise of capitalism and the argument that Europe—being peripheral in the previous stage of mankind's development (that stage which I call 'tributary')—enjoyed a degree of flexibility much higher than the more advanced regions of the East, and therefore could move faster in the new directions opened by the colonization of the Americas.

Reference

Amin, S. (1988). *Eurocentrism*. New York: Monthly Review
Press

The role of Europe in the Early Modern World-System: Parasitic or Generative?

Robert A. Dodgshon

*University College of Wales,
Aberystwyth*

When Columbus set sail across the Atlantic, he expected to find the Orient and found America in its place.
Similarly, Jim Blaut would have us believe that the continent which Columbus left behind was not the place we
thought it to be. This rediscovery of Europe's role within
the early modern world-system inevitably involves the
abandonment of some very basic pre-suppositions. Far
from being a center of innovation and change, a center
whose growth impulses spread outwards to embrace other
parts of the globe, Blaut portrays Europe as having no
internally-derived advantage or edge over other areas. Its
role was parasitic not generative. There is undoubtedly
some benefit in looking at the world-system from an oppo-
site or antipodean viewpoint, seeing it from the perspective of the periphery rather than the core. Yet whilst
making some points of value, Blaut's inversion succeeds
only in flexing, not collapsing, existing structures of interpretation.

A key assumption behind his revisionary approach is
that prior to c.1492, Europe promised no more than other
areas. It had no cultural or deep-rooted predisposition
towards capitalism. Partly at issue here is what Blaut sees
as the Judeo-Christian tendency to treat European history teleologically, to read its direction over a much longer
period than Wallerstein's 'long sixteenth century' as a slow
but inevitable rise to domination. This is too loose a crit-
icism. If scholars have followed Tawney in asserting a link
between religion and the rise of capitalism, then it is a link
founded on the fundamental changes in Judeo-Christian
belief set in motion by the Reformation. The link is historically specific not timeless. We need only read the work
of a writer like Hirschman on the history of Western economic ideas to appreciate the profound ideological changes
that were bound up with the rise of capitalism, changes
that have to be explained within a specific context. Prior
to the early modern period, Hirschman argues, money-
making was treated as a vice nor a virtue, as something
that threatened the established order. By the late eighteenth century, it had become accepted as a source of order
in itself (Hirschman, 1977).

In a more specific critique, Blaut scorns the novel suggestion made in Jones's *European Miracle* (1981) that
because of its less risk-laden environment, Europe had
long been inclined at the margins to translate gains in output into higher levels of material consumption rather than
consume them via increases in population. Personally, I
found this suggestion plausible. More to the point, though,
Jones himself is equivocal over whether its long-standing
drift towards higher levels of material consumption
ensured Europe's pivotal role in the eventual formation
of a 'world-system'. Indeed, if we look at his *Growth
Recurring* (1988), a book that adopts a wider perspective
than *The European Miracle*, we find Blaut's own point
made at some length. Far from seeing European domination as inevitable or a *fait accompli* c. 1492, Jones argues
that quite a number of non-European areas either expe-

rienced or had the potential for rapid economic growth (Jones, 1988: 95 *et. seq*). Mann, likewise, suggests that Europe hardly stood comparison with other areas prior to the late fifteenth century (Mann, 1988: 7). In short, Blaut's rejection of Europe as the inevitable core of an emergent world-system is supported even by some of those he seeks to criticize.

But this point of agreement apart, there still remain significant differences between the world of c.1492 as seen by Blaut and that seen by others. For Blaut, the early growth of capitalism favored no particular region or society. By c. 1492, its seeds were being sown in many different localities. In a sense, he seems inclined to decontextualize the problem by suppressing the way in which some of its basic inputs vary across both time and space. In response, others would concede that the potential for growth was widely scattered but would argue that the realization of this potential was not something synchronized in the way that Blaut would have us believe. Eruptions of growth are always conjunctural, meaning that they depend on the coming together in particular places of a whole variety of factors including the responsiveness of socio-political institutions and their embedded relations, cultural factors, technological innovation and the straightforward opening up of new trading opportunities. Instead of a synchronized world, with widely scattered areas moving in step, we must expect one in which different regional and global configurations of these opportunities are brought to life in a successional way. Jones, for instance, has argued that extensive forms of growth were probably so widespread as to be the norm (Jones, 1988: 150). What mattered was their transformation into what he calls intensive forms (Jones, 1988: 7 and 35). He suggests that over time, a number of societies have probably experienced such growth including ancient Greece, the Abassid caliphate of ninth-century Bagdad, the 10th-13th-century Sung dynasty in China, the Tokugawa shogunate of Japan, 1600-1868, and eighteenth-century Britain (Jones, 1988:

88   1492

35 and 64). Such successive eruptions of growth have been given a strong conceptual context by Ekholm. Civilizations or complex societies, she argues, have always been organized on a core-periphery basis, with new cores or civilizations erupting out of the periphery of former systems. Over time, the scale of such systems may grow larger and the relations between core and periphery, or local and extra-local space, may become more intense but their basic form remains constant (Ekholm, 1980:155-166). Arguably, what was significant about Europe c.1492 was the simple fact that we see, for the first time, the emergence of a core-periphery system that potentially involved interactions on a global scale.

Concerned throughout to expose the Eurocentric posture of much writing, Blaut might respond to this by saying that such reasoning is still teleological, still concerned with explaining how a world-system based on Europe ultimately developed as some kind of final state. His jibe at the concluding remarks of Mann's *Sources of Social Power,* vol. 1, is revealing. Mann talks about successive eruptions of civilization moving westward towards Europe over the late prehistoric and early historic periods. Blaut dismisses this as a typical piece of Eurocentrism as if civilization and the capacity to generate growth was migrating towards its natural hearth. In fact, Mann's vision of sociopolitical structures being continually re-mapped (see especially Mann, 1986: 502 and 538) is consistent with what Jones, Ekholm and others have said (e.g. Braudel, 1977; Dodgshon, 1987). Like them, he would hardly accept that the state of affairs described in his concluding chapters was to remain static. Later volumes will no doubt tell us that the world-system which evolved around western Europe was subject to ongoing change, with the character and scale of interactions being transformed and the core of such a system being continually re-mapped with first Antwerp, then Amsterdam, London, New York and latterly Tokyo serving as its control center. Indeed, the essential flux underpinning these world-systems—a flux that has been increased not decreased by capitalism—is so established in the recent literature that one might be tempted to adapt Andy Warhol's phrase by declaring that given time all regions will be famous for at least fifteen minutes!

Blaut's insistence on a universal rather than localized or historically-specific drift towards capitalism owes much to his dismissal of the idea that different cultures relate to capitalism in different ways. Squeezing human culture c.1492 into some kind of proto-Coca-Cola form is hardly helpful. Whether we see the innate variety of culture as something which capitalism has to negotiate with or simply overwhelm, we gain nothing by assuming that all cultures are equally open or predisposed towards it. A comparison of what Blaut has to say on this matter with the work of someone like Todd shows just how much may be suppressed in his analysis here. Todd has demonstrated brilliantly how different systems of ideology can be linked to different cultural forms and different family structures (Todd, 1985). Given the way in which he articulates this relationship, it is easy to imagine how such differences could embrace the responsiveness of different cultures to the kind of wealth distribution engendered by capitalism and to the institutions involved in achieving such a distribution (e.g. free markets). Interestingly, no less a marketeer than Berry has now acknowledged the formative role which cultural values may play in shaping behavior towards the marketplace even in supposedly modern societies (Berry, 1989). Such variations are deliberately glossed over by Blaut. Thus, at no point does he acknowledge the highly-pertinent work of scholars like Macfarlane on early English family structures and the stress which such work has placed on the early appearance of individualism in English society (Macfarlane, 1978). In view of England's critical role in established views on the rise of capitalism, any argument that demonstrates how such family structures differed not simply from those in, say, Asia, but from those in other parts of

Europe must be answered directly.

Blaut is equally dismissive of any significant role for Europe's varied environment. He seems particularly anxious to discredit the emphasis on environmental factors to be found in *The European Miracle*. For Jones, Europe's mixture of river and forest (river/wold, chalk cheese) environments conferred on it a distinct character, one that favored more localized power structures and more mixed economies when compared with the great riverine empires of the East (Jones, 1981: 9 and 13. Cf. Hall, 1988: 20-21). Blaut sees this as a throwback to older ideas on environmental determinism. The way he prefaces his dismissal of such factors by declaring Jones to be an economic historian—as if this was responsible for his supposed misunderstanding—is unfortunate. As well as being one of the most fertile thinkers on global economic change, Jones is also one of the most productive writers on socio-economic inputs to long-term ecological and biological history. He is more qualified than most geographers to reason out the relation between society and its environment. What is more, his argument is consistent with a great deal of writing on European rural change. Many studies see the local or regional contrast between fertile arable areas and livestock-woodland areas as having a profound effect on their socio-political character. Fertile low-ground areas became associated with a strongly developed feudalism based on lordship, manorialism, demesne production, villeinage and labor services. By contrast, livestock-woodland districts offered less scope for manorialism, desmesne production and labor services simply because—being less fertile—settlement was thinner and arable less important. As Hilton and others have made clear (Hilton, 1969: 17; Postan, 1973: 283), the expansion of settlement into these areas from the 12th century onwards led to free tenures and cash rents, the latter enabling the rent burden to be spread over a greater range of resources. Put bluntly, feudalism responded to variations in available resources by making fundamental adjustments in the nature of landlord-tenant relationships, adjustments which had the effect of forcing tenants into the market. Would this critical early appearance of cash rents and marketing have occurred if local environments had been more uniformly suited to arable farming and demesne production? Nor does the argument end here. Lacking the close social control of feudal areas, livestock-woodland districts experienced rapid population growth over the early modern period and reductions in farm size. As their farm economies became marginalized, many turned to some form of domestic industry and petty production using resources locally available (e.g. wool, timber, leather). Furthermore, as Thirsk noted, the very areas in which domestic industry developed over the 16th-18th centuries became the areas in which the foundations of the Industrial Revolution were later established (Thirsk, 1961: 70-88; Thirsk, 1970: 148-177). The point which I am making is that if Blaut wants us to ignore the significance of Europe's variegated environments, then he needs to confront, and to argue away, a range of debate that is far more extensive and securely-founded in the literature than he perhaps appreciates.

His concern to downplay internal factors behind Europe's position is matched by his concern to emphasize external factors. When distilled down to its most potent essentials, his argument rests on the assumption that Europe's dominant position within the early modern 'world-system' depended on the exploitation of external opportunities. Its role was a mere accident of location not a product of innovatory behavior. His remark that had India been closer to the Americas then it—not Europe— would have seen the primary eruption of capitalism makes this point in a quite startling way. It reduces capitalism to a question of who discovered the Americas first and European society to an expression of locational advantage. Of course, there can be no denying the windfalls which early modern Europe derived from its colonial exploitation of the Americas. The impact of imported gold and silver on its economy has long been an issue of debate and can certainly withstand being raised again in this sort of context. The problem though, is how we gauge its impact. Blaut sees it as a critical source of wealth. Admittedly, when we look at the countries which profited most from the quest for bullion—Spain and Portugal—it enabled marginal elites to indulge in some very conspicuous consumption but, overall, we can hardly conclude that it kickstarted their economies. Indeed, as Ringrose has demonstrated, the activities of the Conquistadores and the free windfall of bullion was followed by the decline not the rise of the Castillian economy (Ringrose, 1989). Blaut's attempt to quantify the labor force involved in colonial production is equally suggestive. Likewise, his proposition that sectors of colonial production like the sugar plantations were major sources of profit rivaling any in Europe is plausible, at least as regards areas like Brazil if not the West Indies. However, much depends on how we draw up the balance sheet and how the considerable costs and risks are discounted. Detailed calculations of the profit generated by English and Dutch trading companies—major participants in the sugar, tobacco and spice trades—suggest modest rather than supercharged profits (e.g. Chaudhuri, 1965).

In the final analysis, though, the scale of wealth generated may not have been the critical factor. As Blaut himself makes clear, what mattered was the fact that colonial wealth was new wealth and in new hands, enabling upstart mercantile elites to rival and outbid traditional elites. This is without question a vital point capable of bearing the weight of argument that he places on it. However, it is also one that can bear a wider if not a different interpretation. As a new source of wealth, as a sector within which new elites could forge new institutions and practices, the colonies were not substantively different from the inner frontier of Europe represented by its livestock-woodland, upland pasture and other marginal areas Each contributed to change in a comparable way. However, the inner frontier of Europe had this extra significance. Put simply, it helped to internalize capitalism within the core of the European state system in a way that the exploitation of the colonies could not hope to do. My point owes much to Polanyi. Early trade for gain, Polanyi argued, was restricted to peripheral centers or ports of trade, where the economic values engendered by trade for gain could not threaten traditional forms of order based on socio-political sources of power (e.g. Polanyi, 1968: 239). Many of the centers and areas where incipient forms of capitalism were to be found c.1492 fall into the category of ports of trade. As peripheral areas whose work practices and ethics of exploitation did not threaten traditional values in the body politic itself, the early colonies were regarded similarly from a European perspective. The really significant change was when overtly commercial values were allowed to insinuate themselves into the core of European state system and when the needs of free trade and private property began to shape state law (cf. Fox, 1971). Such changes were first evident in countries like England and Holland. Without this powerful internal source of change, capitalism would have remained something peripheral, a free-for-all on the edge of otherwise controlled and regulated systems of trade. If by some quirk of continental drift, India had found itself closer to the Americas, the question which Blaut needs to answer is whether its particular socio-political configuration at that moment in time would have allowed it to internalize values which it may have freely tolerated on its periphery.

References

Berry, B. J. L. (1989). Comparative geography of the global economy: cultures, corporations, and the nation–state. *Economic Geography* 65, 11–18.

Braudel, F. (1977). *Afterthoughts on Material Civilization and Capitalism*. Baltimore: John Hopkins University Press.

Chaudhuri, K. N. (1965). *The English East India Company: The Study of an Early Joint–Stock Company*. London: F. Cass.

Dodgshon, R. A. (1987). *The European Past: Social Evolution and Spatial Order*.London: Macmillan.

Ekholm, K. (1980). On the limitations of civilization: the structure and dynamics of social systems. *Dialectical Anthropology* 5, 155–166.

Fox, E. W. (1971). *History in Geographic Perspective*. New York: W. W. Norton.

Hall, J. N. (1988). States and societies: the miracle in comparative perspective. In *Europe and the Rise of Capitalism* (J. Baechler, J. A. Hall and M. Mann eds) pp. 20–38. Oxford: Basil Blackwell.

Hilton, R. H. (1969). *The decline of Serfdom in Medieval England*. London: Macmillan.

Hirschman, A. O. (1977). *The Passion and the Interests: Political Arguments for Capitalism Before Its Triumph*. Princeton: Princeton University Press.

Jones, E. L. (1981). *The European Miracle*. Cambridge: Cambridge University Press.

Jones, E. L. (1988). *Growth Recurring: Economic Change in World History*. Oxford: Clarendon Press.

Macfarlane, A. (1978). *The Origins of English Individualism*. Oxford: Basil Blackwell.

Mann, M. (1986). *The Sources of Social Power, Vol. 1: A History of Power from the Beginning to A.D. 1760*. Cambridge: Cambridge University Pres.

Mann, M. (1988). European development: approaching a historical explanation. In *Europe and the Rise of Capitalism* (J. Baechler, J. A. Hall and M. Mann eds) pp. 6–19. Oxford: Basil Blackwell.

Polanyi, K. (1968). *Primitive, Archaic and Modern Economies*(G. Dalton ed.). Boston: Beacon Press.

Postan, M. (1972). *The Medieval Economy and Society*. London: Weidenfeld and Nicholson.

Postan, M. M. (1973). *Essays on Medieval Agriculture and General Problems of the Medieval Economy*. Cambridge: Cambridge University Press.

Ringrose, D. (1989). Towns, transport and Crown: geography and the decline of Spain. In *Geographic Perspectives in History* (E. D. Genovese and L. Hochberg eds) pp. 57–94. Oxford: Basil Blackwell.

Thirsk, J. (1961). Industries in the countryside. In *Essays in the Economic and Social History of Tudor and Stuart England, in Honour of R. H. Tawney* (F. J. Fisher ed.) pp. 70–88. Cambridge: Cambridge University Press.

Thirsk, J. (1970). Seventeenth–century agriculture and social change. In *Land, Church and People* (J. Thirsk ed.) pp. 147–177. *Agricultural History Review* Supplement No. 18.

Todd, E. (1985). *The Explanation of Ideology: Family Structures and Social Systems. Oxford: Basil Blackwell.*

The European Miracle of Capital Accumulation

R. Palan

The University of Newcastle upon Tyne,

Of all historical events, none generates nearly as much controversy as the rise of Europe to a dominant place in the world. For the European miracle, as it is conventionally called, is a politically loaded question: its study is a mode of self-examination and a way of passing judgment on modern society. What is at stake is not merely the moral values of Western culture and capitalism, but our very sense of historical development as a rational process. In fact, our sense of direction.

The European miracle was first and foremost an 'economic' event: it combined a series of spectacular technological advances with accelerating capital accumulation which thrust the continent briefly (between the French Revolution and the First World War) to an unchallenged position of dominance in the world. Nonetheless, few historical sociologists are prepared to confront the issue of capital accumulation head on. Instead, the whole gamut of cultural, religious, institutional or political factors is scrutinized in great detail, in order, as Blaut (1992) correctly observes, to avoid a simple question: how the process of capital accumulation in Europe finally 'took off'.

In contrast to the tradition which emphasizes the unique role of European rationalism in history (the view that European institutions and culture were the mainstay of European power), which he rightly associates with Eurocentrism, Blaut points to the significance of the year 1492, arguing that the discovery of America opened up a new continent to be exploited at will. The rush of gold and silver into the old continent, and the opening of new markets have acted upon European society which, he contends provocatively, up to that date did not exhibit any unique qualities. Blaut places the stress, therefore, on processes of capital formation in Europe as opposed to any subjective and unproven (some say unprovable) notion of superior cultural traits.

By placing the stress on the process of capital accumulation and, furthermore, in articulating an interesting and sophisticated account of the manner by which the flow of bullion interacted with existing social structures to produce this miracle, Blaut certainly has made an important contribution to the debate. If I have any reservations, however, they are that by placing the stress on capital accumulation, Blaut has tended to neglect a number of unique events which have taken place in Europe.

My feeling is that the reasons for the neglect of certain aspects of the 'European miracle' have more to do with methodology than history: Blaut has certainly done away with the idea of unique European rationality, but he has done so in the name of a rational, ordered and evolutionary concept of history, which is ultimately not so different from the tradition he rejects. As I will try to show in this paper, some of the more sophisticated reflections on the 'European miracle', to be found in writings of Marx and Braudel, sought to escape the .straightjacket of assumption of *rationality of actors* and the *rationality of history* and to favour a more conjunctural, if not chaotic, theory of historical change. These writers share Blaut's conviction that the discovery of America was an event of tremendous significance; nonetheless, in contrast to

Blaut, they believe that the European road to capitalism was unique: after all, capital could have been dissipated and squandered as rapidly as it was accumulated. The discovery of the Americas and the sea routes to Asia may explain the rise of powerful rentier states like the Habsburg empire, which grew ostensibly on the back of American gold. It cannot explain, however, the ever-growing rate of saving and investment in Europe which eventually reached the critical mass and sparked off the industrial revolution.

The Methodology of the European Miracle

The European miracle is commonly discussed in terms of the play of three inter-related methodological variables. To begin with, there are mono-causal, hetero-causal and conjuncture theories. Mono-causal theories maintain that the miracle originated in a specifiable unique cause which is then used to explain what may appear as other causes but are actually effects. Guizot (1985), for instance, regards the fusion of the Hellenic, Germanic and Christian cultures to be of critical importance. Hetero-causal theories maintain that the European miracle was due to a number of inter-related causes. However, as Blaut demonstrates in the case of Weber, these causes are viewed sequentially, as a concatenation of effects, without any attempt to maintain an hierarchy or historical causality between them. Conjuncture theories maintain that the European miracle was due to a number of events which took place at a unique historical conjuncture. The latter stress the uniqueness of history and the lack of any overriding principle of progression.

The second set of variables are endogenous versus exogenous theories of social change. Endogenous theories of social change maintain that the European miracle is explained in terms of internal European dynamics. Exogenous theories of social change maintain that the European miracle was due primarily to development outside Europe and/or to Europe's place in the growing world market.

The third set of variables are normative. The so-called 'Eurocentrics' lay great stress on what they consider to be a remarkable set of institutions and cultures that could have evolved only in Europe. The 'Third World' normative response is typically a version of the famous kettle argument attributed to Freud ('I returned your kettle a couple of years ago . . . anyway it was full of holes . . . I never borrowed a kettle from you'): there is nothing unique about European culture, if there is anything about this culture it is murderous, acquisitive, and lacking in spirituality.

The 'miracle' is portrayed typically as a play of these three variables. 'Idealist' theories which give great prominence to culture tend to be endogenous and Eurocentric. Accordingly, the vast majority of historical sociologists have opted for the straightforward combination:

endogenous - mono-causality- Eurocentricity

Or even the more complicated Weberian version:

endogenous - hetero-causality- Eurocentricity

Blaut criticizes these theories for their neglect of the economic aspect of European development. In spite of Blaut's critique of 'Third Worldism', he attributes the miracle to an articulation of the following variables:

exogenous - mono-causality - Third Worldism

Blaut reverts, in other words, to an alternative play of the same methodological factors. It is regrettable that he neglects two of the more prominent materialist historians,

Marx and Braudel (the latter more of a 'Marxist' than is commonly acknowledged). Both also accorded special place in their narrative to the year 1492. They have developed, however, a far more complicated theory of the European miracle—in effect, breaking with the above combination and seeking a theory that combines endogenous with exogenous theories of social change, and a conjunctural view of historical development. The uniquely 'European' aspect of the miracle, according to these thinkers, is the conjuncture of all these factors. Furthermore, and that is where the real innovation of both Marx and Braudel vis-à-vis their contemporaries, neither viewed the issue in terms of the 'European miracle'; indeed, they have done away with the concept 'Europe' as an heuristic device altogether. I will concentrate on Marx's theory because of the lack of space.

Marx and the European Miracle

In the *Communist Manifesto* Marx put forward the proposition that the world market has expanded primarily due to the discoveries of the sea-routes to America and Asia:

> Modern industry has established the world market, for which the discovery of America paved the way. This market has given an immense development to commerce, to navigation, to communication by land. This development has, in its turn, reacted on the extension of industry (Marx, 1973: 69).

Marx maintained that the discovery of sea-routes was significant because it established the world market. The world market gave immense boost to the growth in transport which in turn 'reacted upon' the extension of industry or capitalism. *Contra* Wallerstein, in Marx's view the world market and capitalism should be viewed as analytically distinct but historically interrelated. They are distinct because the world market *preceded* capitalism. Nonetheless, in the European context, capitalism achieved dominance only through and *because* of the expansion of the world market. The rise of capitalism, therefore, can be explained only in terms of the conjuncture between local conditions and the emerging globalized accumulation process. As I will try to show: it was not 'Europe' that took advantage of the growing world market; indeed, Europe as a geographical entity was incapable of doing so. It was only the political periphery of Europe which was well poised to do so.

In *Capital, Vol. 1* (ch. 31) Marx develops a fuller account of the 'European miracle': an account that, at one and the same time, explains the distinction between capitalism and the world market, and yet conflicts with the stages theory of history which is commonly attributed to Marx.

According to Marx, the middle ages handed down two distinct forms of capital: usurer capital and merchant capital (Marx, 1970: 915). Usurer capital, he maintains, was blocked from becoming industrial capital by the feudal organization of the countryside and the guild organization of the city (p. 915). The new manufacturers could be established therefore only at sea-ports, 'or at points in the countryside which were beyond the control of the old municipalities and their guilds. Hence, in England, the bitter struggle of the corporate towns against these new seed-beds of industry' (p. 915).

Marx argues, in other words, that the 'seeds' of capitalism existed for a long time. The rise of the capitalist mode of production was not an inevitable event, nor was it a case of 'economics' determining 'politics'. On the contrary, it was the well-known breakdown of the feudal order which offered opportunities for merchant capital to develop. Indeed, any discussion which centers on Europe as one huge land-mass misses the crucial point, namely, that capitalism could develop only on the European political periphery, at the point where contemporary political order was at its weakest. It was indeed central to Marx's thought that the rise of capitalism was a 'peripheral' event: it was the conjuncture of the world market with the internal dynamics of the European periphery which explains the rise of the capitalist mode of production to a dominant position. Put differently: without the world market, these peripheral dynamics would have remained what they were all along: peripheral. Without the periphery the 'world market' would have remained a mere pilfering operation soon to fizzle out of its own accord.

The breakdown of the feudal order, says Marx, offered an opportunity for capital to develop. Opportunities, however, do not necessarily translate into practice. The discovery of the sea-routes and the establishment of the world market 'reacted on' these tentative beginnings *accelerating* the trends towards the dominance of the capitalist mode of production. The discovery of sea-routes is viewed by Blaut as an historical accident, partially explained by Europe's geographical location. This is debatable. Columbus was attracted to Madrid because Spain, and in particular, Portugal, were already in possession of a well-established program of marine exploration. Several commentators have noted that the protracted struggle with the Moors contributed to a Spanish society which put a premium on territorial expansion. With the end of expansion within the Iberian peninsula in sight, and with France emerging victorious from the Hundred Years' War, and with the Ottoman Turks making headway in the Mediterranean, Spanish adventurers took to the sea. The 'peripheral' theory of Marx stands even the test of Spain, as a disproportional number of adventurers came from the poor region of Extremadura (which is a desert and has no seashore).

Here was most probably a classic case of an emerging 'virtuous circle': Spanish society was structurally expansive, no doubt, but the fact that the explorations turned out to be successful beyond anyone's wildest dream, acted in turn upon that society, catapulting it into a pivotal role in European history. But the moment Spain ceased from being on the European periphery, its role in the rise of capitalism had virtually ended. John Hall notes that in a similar period and under comparable conditions the Chinese state was able to reassert its authority and nipped capitalism in the bud (Hall, 1986). He concludes that the European competitive system of states gave Europe the edge over its Asian (soon to be) rivals. This ignores the fact that under Philip II and Carlos V—i.e., once the Spanish-Habsburg empire was established as the most powerful state in Europe—it, too, tried its best to nip capitalism in the bud (Trevor-Roper, 1970). A struggle which culminated in the famous, if perennially underestimated, revolt of the Low Lands (Geyl, 1988; Parker, 1977).

The history of Spain shows again that accumulation of capital is an extremely delicate process, and there was better chance that capital will be squandered rather than invested. The fact that in the European context ultimately it was not, cannot be explained in 'political' terms as well: none of the European states, including Holland, can be considered as pro-capitalist. To begin with, there was no capitalist class (as opposed to the bourgeois class—these are not the same thing), to be in support of. Secondly, as Anderson (1974) argues, the strong states, which in contemporary terms meant those that were able to forge close relationships between king and aristocracy, were least likely to support capitalist or proto-capitalist enterprises. Indeed, it was the curious Dutch model of a medieval aristocratic state, forged in Burgundy in 1477 through the concession called the *Grand Privilége*, which gave the local aristocracy-turned-merchants sufficient autonomy to employ the political power of the state for their purposes.

The rise of capitalism was a 'peripheral' development up to the Napoleonic Wars and the industrial revolution—which curiously are viewed as separate events—in two crucial senses: first, it took place among states that were not only geographically on the European periphery, but were marginal to the main military contests of the day—

namely, the struggle between the Habsburgs, the Valois and the Ottoman empires. Secondly, it took place in far-away lands, in obscure battles between merchant-adventurers none of whom had the faintest idea of the significance of their actions.

The 'peripheral' theory of Marx did not contain a clear-cut notion of 'Europe'. Marx did not think in terms of geographical or cultural entities but rather he had a concept of what Gills and Frank (1990) call 'centers of accumulation'. These centers emerged on European soil because Europe was the center of global trading activities.

Each of these centers of accumulation exhibited the familiar cyclical pattern of rise and fall. But, in contrast to the typical cases, the 'European miracle' took place because the fall of one center of accumulation did not engender the termination of the process of accumulation. On the contrary, in Europe, when one center was declining, another appeared and took the torch one step further, so to speak. In Marx's words:

> The different moments of primitive accumulation can be assigned in particular to Spain, Portugal, Holland, France and England, in more or less chronological order. *These different moments are systematically combined together at the end of the seventeenth century in England;* the combination embraces the colonies, the national debt, the modern tax system, and the system of protection (Marx, 1970: 915; emphasis mine)

In the European context, in other words, something unique was happening. The rise and fall of centers of accumulation followed the traditional cycles, no doubt, but it appears that each new center was drawing upon an arsenal of innovatory practices its predecessors had been developing, adding a distinct element of its own.

Marx does not explain how these twin processes of accumulation, the accumulation of institutional practices

(colonies, national debt, modern tax system, system of pro-
tection) and the accumulation of capital, have taken place.
He reverts instead to an Hegelian notion of 'moments' of
history, a notion that explains nothing but is indicative of
non-materialist qualities that kept creeping into his writing. Braudel seems to be one of the rare historians who
have noticed that something unusual was taking place.
what is taken for granted by others, namely, the pan-
European quality of the 'European miracle', is a permanent source of puzzlement to Braudel:

> What is more surprising is that despite the obvious
> time-lags between one country and another, social
> developments, like the familiar economic develop-
> ments they coincided with or expressed, had a ten-
> dency to be synchronized throughout Europe.
> (Braudel, 1979, vol. 2 477).

Conclusions

Braudel again does not explain the pan-European quality of the miracle. He merely notes that it was an unusual event. This is not the place to begin to analyze how this
unique set of events could have occurred. Undoubtedly,
the European state and the European system of states
played an important role. My point is that for a 'materialist' analysis of the European miracle to be successful, it
is not sufficient to accord place of honor to processes of capital accumulation and class structures, nor even to reject
the more chauvinistic aspects of Eurocentrism. Materialist
analysis of the sort that has been advanced by Marx and
Braudel acknowledges that something atypical has happened in Europe, and that the institutional dynamics and
culture must be included in the narrative. Furthermore,
and perhaps more important, no historical event begins
somewhere, sometime, at an identifiable historical point,
as there are no truly self-contained spatio-temporal social

entities (states, civilizations, world-systems). The best form of analysis must, therefore, create an analytical space for historical accidents, experiments and so on. The discovery of America was an important event insofar as it linked with other, perhaps less spectacular, but no less important events.

Acknowledgment

I would like to thank Barry Gills for his helpful comments.

References

Anderson, P. (1974). *The Lineage of the Absolutist State.* London: NLB.

Bendix, R. (1976). *Kings and People: Power and Mandate to Rule.* Berkeley: University of California Press.

Blaut, J. M. (1992). Fourteen ninety–two. *Political Geography* 11(4), pp. 423–453.

Braudel, F. (1979). *Civilization and Capitalism 15th–18th Century,* 3 vols. New York: Harper and row.

Geyl, P. (1988). *The Revolt of the Netherlands,* 1555–1609. London: Cassell.

Gills, B. K. and Frank, A. G. (1990). The cumulation of accumulation: theses and research agenda for 5000 years of world system history. *Dialectical Anthropology* 15, pp. 19–52

Guizot, F. (1985). *Histoire de la civilisation en Europe: Depuis la chute de l'Empire romain jusqu'a la Revolution francaise.* Paris: Hachette.

Hall, J. A. (1986). *Powers and Liberties: the Causes and Consequences of the Rise of the West.* Harmondsworth: Pelican .

Marx, K. (1970). *Capital, Vol. 1.* London: Penguin and NLB

Marx, K. (1973). *The Revolution of 1848.* Harmondsworth: Penguin.

Parker, G. (1977). *The Dutch Revolt.* Harmondsworth:
  Penguin.
Trevor–Roper, H. R. (1971). Spain and Europe 1598–1621.
  In *The New Cambridge Modern History, Vol. IV: The
  Decline of Spain and the Thirty Years' War,
  1609–58/59* (J., P. Cooper ed.) pp. 260–282.
  Cambridge: Cambridge University Press.

Response to Comments by Amin, Dodgshon, Frank, and Palan

J. M. Blaut

I have few disagreements with Amin and Frank, so I will comment first on the Dodgshon and Palan critiques.

Dodgshon

Dodgshon starts by asserting that I wrongly charge that historians argue consistently, teleologically, that Europe has always and necessarily been the most advanced civilization. Most of the historians whom I discuss in the introductory section of the paper do, in fact, take something like this position. For Eric Jones, in *The European Miracle*, non-Europe never had the potential to develop. He doubts that 'indigenous developments were possible' in Africa (Jones, 1981: 156), and in Asia development would have been 'supermiraculous' (238). In *Growth Recurring* he concedes that a non-evolutionary development did occur once or twice in Asia, though not in Africa (Jones, 1988: 91), but evolutionary ('recurring') change results from two permanent European monopolies: (1) a superior environment, and (2) a rationality about sex and procreation: Europeans always showed 'restraint' whereas in Asia 'copulation was preferred above commodities' (Jones, 1981: 15; also see Jones, 1988: 83, 91, 127-129, 141-146, 173-179). Michael Mann does not suggest that (in Dodgshon's words) 'Europe hardly stood comparison with other areas prior to the 15th century'. Mann objects to the 'European self-denigration' implied in Needham's belief that Europe did not overtake China until 1450 (Mann, 1988: 7; also see my review, Blaut, 1989: 444-445). Europe's uniquely rational institutions go back to Iron Age Europe, which Mann contrasts starkly with the despotic Orient (Mann, 1986: chaps. 6-7; Mann 1988, 17). Europe led in technology from the early Middle Ages (7-9,15-17). And Mann is very teleological: Civilization moved its 'leading edge' (17) inexorably north-westward, a sort of westbound Orient Express. '[At] the end of all these processes stood [Great Britain]...perfectly situated...for take-off' (idem). Lynn White, Jr, is even more teleological. Perry Anderson and John Hall invoke ancient European advantages. And so on.

However, as I point out in the paper, many historians today concede that Europe was not at a higher *level* of development than one or two other regions prior to the Middle Ages: the difference, for them, is a matter of rate, or direction. Most of them insist, with Weber, that Europe always had a *potential* not shared by others; not a teleological predestination but an empirical quality of mind or spirit or (rational) social organization, something which would allow Europe, uniquely, to modernize when conditions were ripe. Macfarlane and Todd, whose views Dodgshon chides me for ignoring (or 'suppressing'), make exactly this kind of argument, and both see the potential as going back to ancient times (Macfarlane, 1986: 334ff; Macfarlane, 1978: chap. 1; Todd, 1985:12-13, 100, 197-198). They claim, wrongly in my view, that the traditional kind of West-European family structure was uniquely suited to modernization, capitalism, individualism. This matter of West-Europe's supposedly unique family structure (nuclear, late marriage, birth control) is now, apparently, the most popular version of tunnel history; I did not adequately appreciate that fact when I drafted 'Fourteen Ninety-Two'. Macfarlane thinks this explains the rise of capitalism. Todd thinks it explains the difference between Western democracy and communism, and thinks that Africans and African-Americans don't progress because the African family lacks the father-figure (Todd, 1985: 193). Forgive me if I disagree with Dodgshon and dismiss this family-fetishism as just the latest fashion in Eurocentric history. It is a form of what I call *Euro-Malthusianism:* Western Europeans have always been rational about matters of family, sex, and the like, so they escape the Malthusian disasters which prevent progress everywhere else. (On family structures, birth control, delayed marriage, etc., in other peoples' histories, see, e.g., Berkner, 1989; Cordell and Gregory, 1987; Hassan, 1978; Hilton, 1980; Kertzer, 1989; Lee, 1987; Reid, 1988; Taeuber, 1970).

Dodgshon says that I ignore the role of culture. (Variations in 'cultural values...are deliberately glossed by Blaut'. Blaut 'seems inclined to decontextualise the problem'.) This is a strange charge. Because I deny that European culture is uniquely progressive, uniquely capable of generating capitalism, I am ignoring culture. Does this say that 'culture' must mean 'European culture'? I claim only that the role of culture is no less supportive of development in Africa and Asia than it is in Europe.

According to Dodgshon, I describe the Eastern Hemisphere of 1492 as 'a synchronised world, with widely scattered areas moving in step'. 'Squeezing human culture...into some kind of proto-coca-cola form is hardly helpful'. This is clever verbiage but it does not confront my empirical argument that a number of regions were at comparable levels of development in 1492, or my theoretical argument that human innovativeness was widespread and that constant, intense, criss-cross diffusion spread its fruits across the landscape. And when Dodgshon proclaims the complexity and indeterminacy of the forces involved in development at that period, he is not arguing against my position.

Finally, a brief rejoinder to Dodgshon's empirical points. He thinks that environmental factors favoured European development. He defends Jones' theory that 'because of its less risk-laden environment, Europe...[turned] gains in output into higher...[material wealth] rather than consume them via increases in population'. This is a pair of propositions. Firstly, I doubt that Europe's environment was less risk-laden: Jones gives no good evidence or citation, and, being four times the size of settled Europe, settled Asia might logically have had four times the number of disasters in olden times. Secondly, Jones' assertion that greater environmental risks led Asians to (sociobiologically) procreate rather than accumulate is pure Euro-Malthusianism. Dodgshon then argues that Europe's diversity of environments 'conferred on it a distinct character' favouring small-scale political units and markets as compared with 'the great riverine empires of the East'. Responses-in-brief: (1) Most Asian (and African) environments were quite as diversified as the European. Likewise, social and economic variations across the landscape ('chalk/cheese', etc.) could not have been greater in Europe than in many other places. (2) Those 'empires' did not characterize all or most of 'the East': European political geography was not, at any period, unique in the hemisphere. (3) The argument that Europe's fragmented polities of medieval times somehow favoured modernization is very fashionable (feudalism used to be viewed typically as political chaos, I believe) but the equation of 'empire' with 'stagnation' seems illogical and unsupported. Finally, Dodgshon agrees that accumulation from the periphery was important after 1492, but 'the colonies were not substantively different from the inner frontier of Europe...Each contributed to change in a comparable way'. Wrong. As Walter Prescott Webb pointed out, the New World gave Europeans *six times* as much land as they had previously controlled. To compare this (plus Asia and Africa at later times) with the marginal woodlands and 'upland pastures' of Europe is silly. We are not talking here about abstract peripheries but about a New World.

Palan

Palan points to areas of agreement and disagreement between his view and mine, and this is fair and proper and requires no counter-comment from me. Perhaps I need merely clarify a few of my own points. Indeed I do stress capital accumulation for the rise of capitalism after 1492, but I hope I am not neglecting non-economic aspects of modernization. What I am doing, in essence, is to argue against *both* economic and non-economic theories which claim to explain the rise of capitalism and Europe *before* 1492, and insisting instead that the effect of all such forces was quickened by colonial accumulation. I do not dispute Palan's elegant argument about peripheries, but I think it does not bear on the issues which I raise. (The fact that the center of capitalist development was not in Iberia can perhaps be explained —and often is explained — by the degree to which Italy, Flanders, and some other areas, had already become cores of development prior to 1492.) And I do indeed support an 'evolutionary concept of history'. Not deterministic, but not chaotic. How does this ally me with the Eurocentric historians?

But it is not fair to describe my view as 'mono-causal'. The causal forces in cultural evolution are complex and varied, and this is true everywhere. I fully agree that 'institutional dynamics and culture must be included in the narrative'. What I try to say is this: whatever the causality of evolution toward capitalism and modernity, it has the same complexity everywhere. I advance only a null hypothesis: Europe had no advantage of any sort.

Palan believes that pre-1492 Europe did at least have a few unique advantages. He supports the view that 'the European state and the European system of states' played a unique role. I don't agree. And I don't agree that 'the Chinese state...nipped capitalism in the bud'.

Amin

It should surprise no one that I have no important disagreements with Samir Amin, since my intellectual debt
to him is obvious. There is indeed complementarity
between my argument that Europe had no advantage
whatever prior to 1492 — my null hypothesis — and
Amin's view of development at a global scale. He stops just
short of the null hypothesis, arguing that Europe's marginal location resulted in a slightly less stable, slightly less
indurated, form of the tributary mode of production than
was found elsewhere, and this allowed emerging capitalism (or its ancestor) to develop more easily. I do not think
the tributary mode was more flexible, less indurated, in
Europe. Even Eurocentric historians now talk offhanded-
ly about the political instability of Asian civilizations (e.g.,
Hall, 1988: 29: '[Hindu Indian states] were transient...
Islam had weak polities'). Europe was not the only marginal area, and others seem also to have had comparable
political and social qualities of instability. This was certainly true of Southeast Asia; probably also of sub-Saharan
Africa (see Kea, 1982). If Amin is right about marginali-
ty and its effects, capitalism might logically have appeared
in other marginal zones. The difference between my view
and Amin's is not in itself important but it *becomes* important in the writings of other scholars, including some
Marxist scholars (see Peet, 1991), who claim that Amin's
theory supports their views about Europe's political exceptionalism in the Middle Ages, theories which claim that
the European state and system of states was somehow
more progressive, more open, perhaps more democratic,
than the states of other societies, and that this was crucial for the rise of capitalism in Europe. Some scholars dis-
tort Amin's powerful concept of 'tributary mode of
production' and, in like manner, try to use it to support
European exceptionalism by declaring 'feudalism' to be
that sub-species of the tributary made which, in Europe,
had greater potentiality for transformation into capitalism based on political openness or greater development

of rent as against taxation (Wickham, 1988). Mainly to avoid such propositions, I use 'feudal mode' in preference to its synonym, 'tributary mode'.

Frank

Andre Gunder Frank's contribution is a serious theoretical essay on large questions of world-scale cultural evolution, rather than merely a comment on my paper. Here I will only comment briefly on a few of Frank's points which bear on the argument of my paper.

Why was fourteen ninety-two a break-point in cultural evolution? Basically, because the shock of contact between the two hemispheric segments of the human population, after millennia of almost total isolation, produced sudden and massive changes in the rate of development of the world system: specifically, hastening the crumbling of the feudal or tributary mode of production and the rise of capitalism. (I do not agree with the diffusionists who believe that Western Hemisphere civilization owes anything important to precolumbian diffusion across either the Atlantic or the Pacific: agriculture, class society, states, and civilization as a whole were developed by Americans on their own. Frank should agree with this although his comment about early transpacific contacts is a bit baffling.)

As to the age of the world system, I would start earlier than Frank suggests. I suspect that class stratification was implicit in the Agricultural Revolution — though it is also possible that class preceded and engendered agriculture — and I think that both agriculture and the earliest class states were to be found in many parts of the Eastern Hemisphere, not only in and near Mesopotamia (Blaut, 1987). Rapid, constant, criss-cross diffusion was spreading these innovations all across the hemisphere at all times. Of course there were, in all ages, centers and peripheries, and of course the supremacy of one center gave way ('musical chairs') periodically to another. This generalization does not, however, give us an empirical explanation for the rise of the European center at one special conjuncture. And my argument fully comprehends this generalization; in 1492 there were a number of centers at comparable levels of development and moving at comparable rates in comparable directions (toward something like capitalism); also, a number of peripheries.

I cannot, however, abandon the idea of qualitative transformations in the world system in favour of Frank's concept of continuity. He is quite right in seeing the Marxian concept of sequential revolutionary transformations as a projection (rightly or wrongly) of Marxian hopes for a socialist revolution. But capitalism is not feudalism and a bourgeois revolution did take place. I do not date the latter from 1492. I think we must describe a transformation of class society from a landlord-dominated (tributary, feudal) mode of production centered on agricultural production into a new mode in which the urban division of labour, the urban ruling class, and non-agricultural production created a new form of society, with new classes (rural and urban) above and below. This is capitalism. Its sprouts can perhaps be found in very early times. Doubtless it dominated a few small polities in the Middle Ages. I believe the genuine revolutionary transformation was the acquisition of *political power* by the new ruling classes on a *large scale*, over large societies and large landscapes: the Bourgeois Revolutions of the 17th and 18th centuries. As I say in the last part of my paper, the subsequent industrial revolution as a technical and economic transformation was broadly implicit in this *political* transformation. (So much for economic determinism.) However, the Bourgeois Revolutions occurred in Europe because of colonialism after 1492: the non-European landscapes provided the first large-scale control of territory, and gave a great boost to the bourgeois classes (plural) in their efforts to gain political control in Europe. Would capitalism-as-we-know-it have appeared in the world if there had been no '1492' (colonial accumulation)? I have no idea. Certainly a mode of production dominated by a not-entirely-rural ruling class would have emerged, though much later, and goodness knows where.

Gunder Frank has been fighting against Eurocentric social science for three decades; his early work influenced my first formulation of the ideas put forward in the present paper (Frank, 1967, 1969; Blaut, 1970), I am surprised that he now considers it somewhat unimportant (and unworthy) to fight against these Eurocentric theories. They are still the ruling ideas; Needham and Abu Lughod and Amin and Frank have not overthrown them. Even in radical thought, the Brenners and Andersons and Laclaus are still being taken more seriously than the Franks and Amins and Wallersteins: the former are producing ideas compatible with the ruling ideas, the latter not. So critique of the history and nature and structure of Eurocentric ideas is probably as important as the production of new and non-Eurocentric theory. And it is more fun to do.

References

Berkner, L. (1989). The stem family and the developmental cycle of the peasant household. *American History Review* 77, 398-428.

Blaut, J. (1970). Geographic models of imperialism. *Antipode* 2, 65-85.

Blaut, J. (1987). Diffusionism: A uniformitarian critique. *Annals of the Association of American Geographers*, 77, 3047.

Blaut J. (1989). Review of J. Baechler, J. Hall, and M. Mann, eds, *Europe and the Rise of Capitalism*. Progress in Human Geography 13, 441-448.

Cordell, D. and Gregory, J., eds. (1987). *African Population and Capitalism: Historical Perspectives* Boulder: Westview.

Frank, A. (1967). *Capitalism and Underdevelopment in Latin America*. New York: Monthly Review Press.

Frank, A. (1969). Sociology of development and underdevelopment of sociology. In his *Latin America:*

Underdevelopment or Revolution New York: Monthly
Review Press, pp. 21-94.

Hall, J. (1988). States and societies: The miracle in historical perspective. In *Europe and the Rise of Capitalism*.
(J. Baechler, et al. eds). Oxford: Blackwell.

Hassan F. (1978). Demographic archeology. In *Advances in
Archeological Method and Theory*, vol. 1., M. B.
Schaffer, ed.

Hilton R. (1980). 'Individualism and the English peasantry. *New Left Review* no. 180, 111-114.

Jones, E. L. (1981). *The European Miracle*. Cambridge:
Cambridge University Press

Jones, E. (1988). *Growth Recurring: Economic Change in
World History*. Oxford: Clarendon.

Kea, R. (1982). *Settlements, Trade, and Polities in the
SeventeenthCentury Gold Coast*. Baltimore: Johns
Hopkins Press.

Kertzer, D. (1989). The joint family household revisited:
Demographic constraints and household complexity in
the European past. *Journal of Family History* 14, 1-16.

Lee, G. (1987). Comparative perspectives. In: *Handbook of
Marriage and the Family*, (M. Sussman and S.
Steinmetz, eds). New York: Plenum.

Macfarlane A. (1986). *Marriage and Love in England:
1300-1840*. Oxford: Blackwell.

Macfarlane, A. (1978). *The Origins of English
Individualism*. Oxford: Blackwell.

Mann, M. (1986). *The Sources of Social Power, vol. l: The
History of Power from the Beginning to A.D. 1760*.
Cambridge: Cambridge University Press.

Mann, M. (1988). European development: Approaching a
historical explanation. In *Europe and the Rise of
Capitalism* (J. Baechler, et al., eds). Oxford: Blackwell,
pp. 6-19..

Peet R. (1991). *Global Capitalism: Theories of Societal
Development*. London: Routledge.

Reid, A. (1988). *Southeast Asia in the Age of Commerce:
1450-1680*, vol. 1. New Haven: Yale.

Taeuber, I. (1970). The families of Chinese farmers. In

Family and Kinship in Chinese Society (M. Freedman, ed). Stanford: Stanford University Press..

Todd, E. (1985). *The Explanation of Ideology*. Oxford: Blackwell.

Wickham, C. (1988). The uniqueness of the East. In *Europe and the Rise of Capitalism* (J. Baechler, et al., eds). Oxford: Blackwell, pp. 66-100.

INDEX